T0352899

THE SCYTHING HANDBOOK

IAN MILLER

THE SCYTHING HANDBOOK

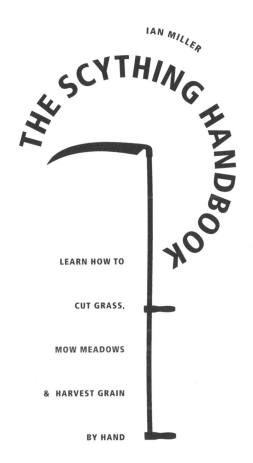

LEARN HOW TO

CUT GRASS,

MOW MEADOWS

& HARVEST GRAIN

BY HAND

filbert *press*

For my daughters Iantha and Vivien

Published in 2016 by
Filbert Press Ltd
filbertpress.com

Please note: great care has been taken to ensure that the information
contained in this book is both accurate and complete. However, since the skills
and competence of individuals vary widely, and no book of this nature can
replace specialist advice where appropriate, neither the author nor the
publisher can accept legal responsibility or liability for any loss or damage
caused by reliance on the information.

Printed in China

ISBN: 978-0-9933892-4-5

A catalogue record for this book is available from the British Library.

The longer Levin mowed, the oftener he felt the moments of unconsciousness in which it seemed not his hands that swung the scythe, but the scythe mowing of itself, a body full of life and consciousness of its own, and as though by magic, without thinking of it, the work turned out regular and well-finished of itself. These were the most blissful moments.

LEO TOLSTOY

Contents

Foreword

About a dozen years ago, while reading Mother Earth News, an American magazine and website devoted to sustainable living, I came across a feature on mowing with a European-style scythe. I had always been intrigued by the long blades and curvaceous handles of scythes, and had even borrowed one from a friend, but it didn't seem to work – or I had never acquired the right technique. This author, however, said the European blade was completely different: lighter, sharper, easier to use.

I have only rarely been persuaded to buy anything without seeing or trying it first, and the price (more than $100 for the kit) would strain my budget. So I called the author, who ran a mail-order business called Scythe Supply. I was, of course, sceptical about what I assumed would be a sales pitch, but Elliott Fishbein was not a salesman. He was a fine carpenter who had fallen in love with a new/old tool, and started the business as a way to share the joys of a different kind of handiwork.

He asked me as many questions as I asked him – maybe more. By the end of our conversation, he had convinced me not to buy his longest blade (longer does not equal better). Instead, he sold me an 18 in (45 cm) ditch blade, which he assured me would suit all my needs. I needed only to cut a little grass and lots of blackberry (in Western Oregon, where I live, Himalayan blackberry is a gardener's bane, usually attacked with poison or machetes; short of goats, however, the scythe is the ultimate weapon against these tough, spiky and rambunctious invaders).

That conversation transformed mere shopping into an act of faith and friendship. The scythe arrived. Despite my utter lack of experience and knowledge, it worked as well as promised. I was hooked, sold, convinced – and happy! Joyfully, I mowed my patches of grass and easily took out swathes of blackberry, without losing any blood! After a few hours of practice, I was keen to challenge my neighbour's noisy petrol-powered strimmer with the deadly whispers of my ditch blade. I eagerly read *The Scythe Book* by David Tresemer, which Elliott had recommended (at the time, the only book to deal with this tool). Sharpening and peening (which Ian demystifies, see pp. 52-69) were challenges I met with zeal. Elliott answered my phone calls and questions with information and encouragement. In gratitude (and because it was about bread and baking, and thus also grains) I sent him a copy of a little how-to book I'd written on using earth to build a wood-fired bread oven. And when I read one of Tolstoy's stories about an aristocrat who goes out mowing with 'his' peasants and comes alive with the joy of it, Elliott added the quote to his list of literature links.

A year or two later Elliott's wife wrote to let me know that he had died, tragically, in a car crash, but the friendship continued as Carol carried on the business from their home in Maine. The scythe remains my favourite garden tool, but as we've never had the acreage to keep animals, much less plant pasture, I've not yet had the opportunity to try the kind of hay-making that Ian describes in his book. Perhaps one day. Until then, every garden visitor gets an introduction to the scythe. Twice I've been invited to the local agricultural college to demonstrate or teach mowing to students interested in sustainable agriculture and petro-free methods.

This wonderful tool offers many possibilities which, as Ian suggests, go much further than simply 'mowing the grass'. What you learn from mowing with a scythe can indeed change your relationship to the land, and thereby your life. The nature of technology (from the Greek root tekne, meaning art, craft, or skill) is to shape what and how you learn by changing how you work in and with the world. A scythe shifts your awareness away from noisy machines to your body, the feel of the sun or rain on your back and the condition of the grass itself, as well as the blade and your muscles. As tool (and technique) organize the grass in a windrow, the work of collecting it grows more obvious. Instead of haphazardly scattered 'waste' needing 'disposal', you might begin to see it as valuable stuff: feed for a family cow, or for rabbits or chickens, or merely for all the hungry organisms in your compost pile.

Mowing with a scythe teaches much more than simply how to make grass shorter. It teaches the value of labour, both as a way to make a living and as a source of pleasure, strength and skill. If you find others with whom to share those values, that living, those pleasures, strengths and skills, you will find that your community (your 'dwelling place') will grow as well (and as beautifully) as your garden.

Like Ian, I imagine scythe-wielding corps of enthusiastic, competent, strong mowers who can joyfully displace the loud, lonesome and very expensive mowing machines used to batter roadside weeds and brush into chips and dust. I imagine a new kind of landscape contracting that sees lawns as pastures, and 'mowing the grass' as feeding cows to give us milk and cheese. (Indeed, this vision is inspired in part by stories from Jaime Lerner in Curitiba, Brazil, where city government replaced their municipal parks with shepherds and sheep.) I imagine homeowners trading rights to their grass in return for a share of milk and meat. I imagine mowing parties that celebrate harvest by making their windrows into labyrinths in the fields. I imagine a new generation of blacksmiths relearning the art of forging long, light blades. None of this vision suggests a retreat from modernity – instead, it offers choices based on a complexity of real values, rather than on the mathematical simplicity of 'economics'.

If you do decide to try out scything after reading this book, take Ian's advice and look for a buddy with more experience to make it a shared endeavour. There's pleasure and wisdom in numbers, as well as strength and safety.

Kiko Denzer

Introduction: my story

'Buried among the things we hate is a class of products that are in that class only because they are weird. They make us nervous. They are sufficiently different that it takes us some time to understand that we actually like them.' MALCOLM GLADWELL, *BLINK*

I imagine a bit of eye-rolling when people come across this book while looking through titles on farming, gardening or self-sufficiency at a library or bookshop. I admit that on the surface it might look like a glorification of Luddites or perhaps some kind of gimmick, but my aim here is to present what I have come to see as a perfectly legitimate and reasonable choice for homeowners, farmers and others who are looking to save money, reduce their use of fossil fuels, be less dependent on industrial products, take better care of their land, increase their autonomy, get to know their bodies and land better, and stop using noisy, dirty machines.

Here's how I got into working with scythes and why I think your life will be better when you start using one. My first significant exposure to a scythe was an indirect one. In the late 1990s and early 2000s, I was a transplant from Iowa to San Francisco in my twenties, trying to get a music career going. Young and on my own for the first time, it was important for me to show the world that I was in charge of my life and one of the ways I set about doing that was to get tattoos. After getting a couple, one of which I liked, the other not so much, I got an idea for the perfect tattoo: I knew that at some point in my life I had seen woodcut art of people

working in fields with hand tools. With this vague notion in mind, I started spending weekends at the public library, poring over art books in hopes of finding such an image. After more than a year of looking and finding nothing that spoke to me, I pretty much gave up on it.

Around this time, after a few bad band breakups and lots of wheel-spinning, I became disillusioned about playing music for a living and fell in love with the idea of becoming an organic farmer. Despite having grown up in Iowa, typically the state with the highest corn production in the US, I had neither experience nor any connection with farming or gardening, so I started looking at the public library's selection of books on these subjects. One day I typed the words 'agricultural technology' into the library's search engine and the book *Dream Reaper* by Craig Canine came up. I found it on the shelf, started leafing through it, then said, 'Wait a minute!' and looked again at the front cover. It was a woodcut of a man cutting a grain harvest with a scythe. That was it – just the image I'd been looking for over the last two years. A few days later I had it on my arm and had learned from the tattoo artist how to pronounce the word 'scythe'. That was late 2001. The path to becoming an organic farmer that I figured

The use of the scythe has never died out in mountain areas. Now urbanites, permaculturists and others by the thousand are rediscovering the efficiency and usefulness of this remarkable tool.

out for myself was to go back to college, so I studied agroecology at UC Santa Cruz. As a result of that course, I did an internship on a biodynamic farm in south-central Austria for six months in 2005. Within the first few days of being there I saw their scythe hanging in the workshop and I immediately knew I had to learn how to use that thing. I tried it out a few times, hacking at some weeds, having no idea what I was doing. My only points of reference were swinging a baseball bat or a golf club, neither of which are relevant to using a scythe. I would quickly get tired and very little of what I swung at was actually cut. I had no doubt that there was more to it than meets the eye, but I couldn't imagine how to use it more effectively. However, it didn't take long to realize that there is practically no such thing as a farm without a scythe in Austria.

That summer, there was a Romanian worker on the farm. Florin was a year my junior, but he was light years ahead of me in terms of experience on farms. He could do everything. I used to wake up to the sound of a whetstone sliding across the blade in the early morning before he mowed grass for a small flock of sheep whose paddock had too little forage. Florin seemed to put almost no effort into mowing a surprisingly large amount of grass.

Before I knew it, the internship was over and the only scything experience I got were those few times breaking a lot of sweat to cut very little grass. After graduating, I returned to the farm in early 2006, and in spring 2007 I discovered that there was an organization that offered tuition in mowing with the scythe. I took a half-day mowing lesson,

bought a scythe (which I still use today) and talked neighbours into letting me mow their apple orchard, which was at least 1 acre (0.4 ha) large. It took me about a week, as I recall, but I mowed the whole thing, feeding the daily harvest to their pigs.

While in Austria, I fell in love with the whole-grain rye sourdough bread that we ate every day at the farm. I learned how to bake it and eventually started to dream about growing and harvesting grains using only hand tools, then baking bread with the grain and selling it to earn my living. A move back to my native Iowa in late summer 2007 provided me with the chance to do just that.

While on what was intended to be a two-week visit to Iowa in August 2007, I drove up to Decorah to visit Seed Savers Exchange, a non-profit organization dedicated to maintaining heirloom vegetables. On a whim, I decided to take a résumé along with me, fully expecting that there was no chance of getting a job at a well-known place with such a great reputation. To my surprise, they were interested in me, so I took up a job with Seed Savers and while there met an older homesteading couple, back-to-the-landers from the 70s, who were intrigued by my ideas and said I could try them out on their land. I bought Kiko Denzer's *Build Your Own Earth Oven*, followed the instructions therein and started baking bread and selling it at the farmers market. Not too long after that, I had a neighbour plough and seed 1 acre (0.4 ha) with rye and ½ acre (0.2 ha) with spelt.

Around July 2009, it was time to harvest. I had been at the farmers market for almost a year at that point and wasn't getting rich, but I was selling everything I could bake. Now I was finally going to realize the last piece of the dream.

I had engaged the help of a local woodworker to build a grain cradle for one of my scythes. This is an attachment designed to gather the cut grains and lay them on the ground in an orderly way for easy binding. Mine was one of the big rake-style cradles that I knew from pictures from the Depression. So there I stood on a cool, dewy morning at the edge of a field of rye, about to start harvesting with the most traditional equipment you could imagine. I even made a short video, where I said something like 'Today is the first day of the rest of my life.' It really felt like an important moment for me and I reflected on how long it must have been since small grains had been harvested with a scythe in Winneshiek County, Iowa. Then the first swing: the whole thing, blade and cradle, lodged in the dense stand of rye stalks. Okay, think about it, make a few adjustments, try again. Same result. No matter how hard I tried, there was no way to move the scythe through the grain without everything getting tangled up. I changed the angle, changed the placement, changed the length – nothing helped. My dream was crumbling before my eyes.

A day or two later, I contacted Botan Anderson, a fellow scything enthusiast in Wisconsin who imports the top-quality scythes from Austria that I use. He mentioned a two-stroke technique that he had heard of, where the first stroke cuts the grain, then a second stroke in the same spot collects the grain and sweeps it to the ground on your left. I tried it the next day . . . it worked!

It took three days and I had some help from friends who came to tie bundles of grain into sheaves and lean them into each other to form stooks for curing in the field. Finally, I had my harvest.

A large garden or small farm without a scythe almost guarantees extensive use of petrol-burning machines such as strimmers, lawnmowers and tractors. As I see it, the only reason not to have a scythe is if you are unaware of their existence, their purpose and how pleasant they can be to use. I no longer grow enough grain to sell bread for a living, but I still grow grains for my own use and make hay by hand.

Through chance, curiosity and concerted effort, I have learned a lot about scythes and scything, and I'd like to share this knowledge with you here in the hope of inspiring as many of you as possible to choose the right technology to help you meet all your needs.

Unless I indicate otherwise, when I use the word scythe I am referring to a forged Austrian scythe (sometimes called a European or continental European scythe). There are hundreds, if not thousands, of designs for scythe blades and there is a fair amount of variety even among Austrian blades. American and English scythes are stamped (and thus not possible to peen), and were developed to harvest sugar cane and reed and are therefore not suitable for hay and small grain harvesting.

The directions on using a scythe are given for right-handed people. If you are left-handed and using a scythe built for mowing left-handed, simply reverse them.

Ian Miller

CHAPTER 1 | HOW SCYTHING WILL CHANGE YOUR LIFE

Imagine a town or suburb where nobody has a lawn mower. Walking along on a Saturday morning, from time to time you hear the sound of a whetstone being dragged across metal, a bit like a knife being sharpened, but duller, softer. Later in the day, you walk by again and see cut grass spread evenly across lawns and the occasional haycock, proudly displayed in the front garden, destined for pets and livestock, mulch for the garden or the compost pile.

Now imagine a cluster of small-holdings or small farms where nobody has a tractor. On most days during the growing season, farmers wake up to milk their animals and move them along to the next paddock. But first, before the morning dew has evaporated, they grab their scythes, hone them and do an hour or so of mowing before spreading the grass out to cure and collecting some for the animals to munch on during milking. That evening the farmers hang the grass up on a quadripod or Swedish-style wire rack so that water is shed should it rain. In a week or two, depending on the weather, the finished hay is loaded onto a cart and dumped into the hayloft in the barn, to be dropped down to livestock as needed over the winter.

In midsummer, a patch of small grains, maybe up to 1 acre (0.4 ha) or so, is cut, bound and stooked by these farmers, now working together, then threshed and winnowed a few weeks later with a treadle-powered thresher they chipped in to buy together. Undersown grasses and clovers then take over the patch, returning it to meadow. Animal impact, mostly from pigs, establishes the seed bed in the next acre of meadow for the following year's crop of small grains.

The scythe and the techniques involved with it come from traditional Alpine farming, which is based on local production for local needs. It improves the soil, increases biomass, prevents erosion and makes for extremely high-quality foods. It involves meaningful work that is creative, challenging and invigorating. In an age where climate change is upon us, the scythe is a technology that is relevant and useful to us all.

At this point you might think that if it is so easy and pleasant to make hay and grow grains yourself, why aren't more people doing it already? One explanation is the ubiquitous assumption that the latest, most high-tech solution is necessarily the best one. But, for example, the existence of cars doesn't mean that bicycles are irrelevant. Both are forms of transportation, yet they meet completely different needs. Replacing your lawnmower with a scythe is much like the experience you may have when choosing to ride your bike to work: exhilaration, rejuvenation and increased energy and confidence.

What will I use my scythe for?

A scythe can tackle a wide range of jobs efficiently, which means you may be able to dispense with a range of garden tools that aren't in everyday use. You can use it, for example, to mow grass in awkward places such as alongside walls and fences, or on slopes and wet ground that is inaccessible to heavy machinery. Once you have acquired the technique, a scythe is a joy to use and provides a wonderful experience for mind and body.

MOWING THE LAWN If you have a lawn to mow, you may only be familiar with these choices for getting the job done: a petrol or electric lawn mower or a hand mower. They are generally effective, but are expensive and noisy. Petrol mowers are also incredibly polluting, emitting more polycyclic aromatic hydrocarbons – probable carcinogens – than a car, increasing ground levels of lung-irritating ozone and emitting carbon dioxide.

To eliminate air and noise pollution, you can use a scythe instead to mow the lawn. You'll have to let your lawn grow longer than you may be accustomed to for the scythe to be effective, but this also means mowing less frequently. Make hay with the cuttings for backyard livestock such as chickens and rabbits, or use them as a mulch or in the compost bin.

MOWING A WILDFLOWER MEADOW In prairie and wildflower plantings, the scythe can be used to remove problem plants (such as wild parsnip or the saplings of unwanted trees) without causing large amounts of damage either at the point of use or by bringing equipment in and out. Strategically timed, larger-scale mowings can help to encourage desired plants and discouraged those that are not wanted.

MULCHING Ask a gardener who does not mulch why this is and the response is likely to be that they do not know what they would use, that it is too expensive or that they don't want to haul bales of hay or straw. Meanwhile their garden is in the middle of a free source of mulch, if they only had the knowledge and tools to tap into it. The benefits of mulching cannot be overstated. Mulch suppresses weeds and retains moisture so you need to weed and water less; it covers the soil, thereby preventing erosion, hardpan and the splash back that encourages the spread of soil-borne diseases; it insulates the soil, allowing you to keep root crops in the ground longer; and it ultimately adds organic matter to the soil.

Furthermore, being able to make your own mulching material for free makes it easy to use no-till gardening techniques such as sheet mulching, lasagna gardening or no-dig beds which require mulch and compost. Turning the soil is one of the worst things you can do to it as it mixes upper layers of soil into lower layers and vice versa. Different layers of soil have different forms of soil life and you ultimately destroy soil organic matter and make hardpan more likely. By abandoning tillage and planting directly into a sheet mulch that consists of sheets of newspaper and/or cardboard applied directly to the top of the soil to kill and inhibit weeds plus compost, hay and/or straw on top of the sheet layer, you allow soil microfauna to aerate, loosen and fertilize the soil for you. This creates a win-win situation as it is much better for the soil and is much less work.

COMPOSTING Different sources give varying estimates of the carbon-nitrogen ratio of hay; they range from 25:1, which is in the ideal composting range of 25–30:1, all the way up to 50:1. In general, the more clover or other nitrogen-fixing plants in the hay, the higher the nitrogen content will be. For a diverse lawn, with perhaps fescue and some crab grass, ground ivy, plantain and a little white clover, it's a safe bet that it's closer to 50:1. Hay made from a field of primarily alfalfa and/or red clover is probably closer to 25:1. Hay from your lawn piled alternately with food scraps and manure from backyard livestock will make for fantastic compost. Note that dried hay has a significantly higher C:N ration than freshly cut grass, which is closer to 10:1.

MAKING HAY Hay is an under-appreciated resource for gardeners and small farmers, probably because it is thought of as something that is only made with expensive machinery in huge fields. The scythe is the original grass-harvesting tool and it leaves the entire blade of grass intact above the cut from the crown of the plant. Grass cut in this manner can be dried in the sun and wind to make hay, which is incredibly useful for home gardening and for keeping backyard chickens or other livestock.

FEEDING LIVESTOCK AND PETS
Whether you have a few chickens, a horse, a milk cow or a small herd of goats or sheep,

winter fodder and bedding can be the biggest challenge and expense. But if you are making hay from your own lawn by using a scythe, your hay is not only as local as it gets, it is also free. This means you can produce your own eggs, milk (and by extension butter and cheese) and other animal products of the highest quality for very little money.

GROWING GRAIN Small grains are an overlooked crop in the home garden and allotment as well as on small farms. If you are interested in grains other than wheat for baking your own bread, such as emmer, einkorn, spelt, or khorasan wheat – all of which are more nutritious, though lower

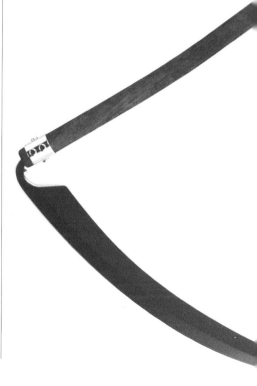

yielding than wheat – you'll be able to save money by growing your own. Your grain will essentially be free (think free bread and free chicken feed), you can control how it is grown (free of industrial chemicals, in a polyculture, with no use of fossil fuels, adapted to your local conditions) and you will have a deep-rooted, light-feeding addition to your crop rotation.

To achieve a worthwhile yield in the amount of space available in a home garden, you will probably need to maximize the yield per square foot. The highest yields possible – up to 50 lb (22.7 kg) from about 200 sq ft (18.5 m²), which is about enough for 1½ lb (700 g) of bread per week – are those achieved through bio-intensive gardening, which means growing grain in double-dug beds with lots of added compost. Or, if you have more space and don't need to have such high yields per square foot, you can use animals such as chickens or pigs to till and fertilize the soil for you. At the field scale, small grains make for a perfect nurse crop for establishing a hay field.

PRODUCING STRAW When you grow your own grains and harvest with the scythe, you also get the long straw that is the seed stalk of the plant. Straw is an immeasurably useful product for the garden and small farm. It is a perfect 'brown' ingredient for the compost pile, ideal bedding for livestock and an excellent weed-free mulch material.

GARDENING Whether you garden at home, in an allotment, a community garden or elsewhere, you can use the scythe for quietly performing many tasks with ease. Mow a stand of green manure; clear beds of vegetation; keep paths or border areas mown; and mow marginal areas near fences, gates or walls.

When you step back and look at all you could be doing with the scythe, it may suddenly seem like an indispensable tool for the home and garden. Using a scythe can certainly help you achieve a lot around your lawn, garden or meadows and at a speed that you might find surprising for a hand tool.

CHAPTER 2 THE SCYTHE AND HOW TO USE IT

The movements and techniques involved in mowing with a scythe are very simple, but not necessarily easy to perfect. While I hope that this chapter will equip you to go out and use your scythe, there's no substitute for observing an experienced practitioner and having him or her offer feedback on your own technique or physically guide you through the motions. Consequently, if you can find a teacher too, don't miss the chance for some on-the-spot learning.

There are subtle differences in scythes from one manufacturer to another, but any scythe calling itself an Austrian or European scythe ❶ will consist of the following components: the blade; the scythe ring, which holds the blade to the snath, the instrument used to hold the blade at the appropriate angle and move it through the grass; and the grips, which may or may not be removable and/or adjustable.

The blade itself ❷ has various areas, each with its own name and importance to the mower. The cutting edge is single-bevelled and, as you might expect, is the part that actually cuts the grass; the chine gives rigidity to the entire blade and is what, in addition to the person using the scythe, guides the blade through the grass in a semi-circle; the point of the blade is angled up from the ground when the scythe is in use; the beard is where the edge ends nearest to the snath; and the tang, with its heel and knob, is the part of the blade that connects with the snath and scythe ring and establishes the angle between blade and snath.

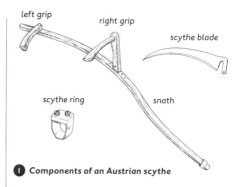

❶ **Components of an Austrian scythe**

Scythe Assembly

For snaths with one or more detachable grips, start the assembly of the scythe by mounting the grips. Ideally, their position will be adjustable, as they are on the Swiss-made Upper Austrian snath shown here. Notice how the design prevents them slipping along the length of the snath or twisting ❸. To adjust the position of the grips to your body, hold the scythe next to you with the blade end on the ground ❹. The right (lower) grip should be at about hip or belt level. The distance to the left grip should be a bit more than the distance from

❷ *A forged Austrian scythe blade*

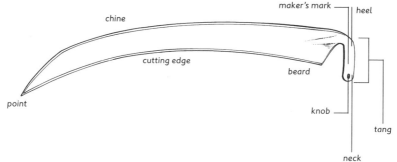

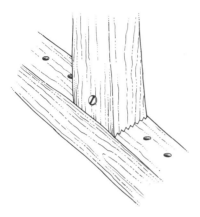

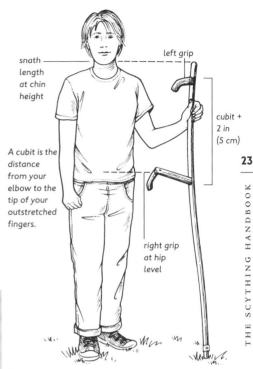

snath
length
at chin
height

A cubit is the
distance
from your
elbow to the
tip of your
outstretched
fingers.

left grip

cubit +
2 in
(5 cm)

right grip
at hip
level

4 *Fitting the scythe to your body*

your elbow to the tip of your outstretched
fingers. To measure, place the back of your
elbow (the bottom of your upper arm)
on the right grip and reach up to the left
grip with an open hand. The left grip
should be 1¼–2 in (3–5 cm) from your
fingertips. Adjust both grips accordingly
and tighten firmly.

To attach the blade, first put the scythe
ring around the end of the snath and slide
it past the knob receptacle. Then place the
tang of the blade on the snath so that the
knob at the bottom of the tang inserts into
the knob receptacle on the snath. Finally,
slide the scythe ring up to the neck of the
tang and tighten the screws of the scythe
ring to attach the blade to the snath, leaving
them loose enough to allow you to adjust
the hafting angle more precisely **5** .
Tighten each screw a little at a time, rather
than completely tightening one before
moving on to the next, to ensure uniform
tightness and a secure fit.

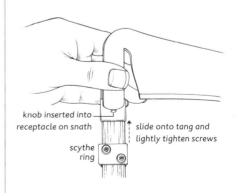

knob inserted into
receptacle on snath

scythe
ring

slide onto tang and
lightly tighten screws

5 *Attaching the blad to the snath*

Place scythe on the ground and left grip against lower shin.

To ensure that the edge of the blade makes contact with grass at the correct angle, the tang angle may need some adjustment. This is the angle formed by the displacement of the tang from parallel with the beard when viewing the blade from the side, which is typically 25–30 degrees.

Ultimately, the edge of the scythe blade should be coming up from the ground to cut grass at an upward angle when the scythe is held in the mowing position described below, and the edge will be about ⅜ in (10 mm) above the ground **8**. Insert a wedge between the snath and tang as necessary **9**.

To adjust the hafting angle (that is the angle of the blade to the snath as you mow, which is defined by how far away from parallel the tang is to the snath), place the left grip against the bottom of your shin, with the blade on the ground and the scythe laid out straight ahead of you **6**. Note the position of the beard in relation to some marker on the ground, such as a twig. Using the right grip, swing the scythe to the right, keeping the left grip on the base of your shin, until the point of the blade is where the beard was. Where is the point in relation to the twig? Typically, for grass mowing, the point will be about three finger-widths below the beard **7**. Adjust accordingly, by shifting the orientation of the tang closer to or farther from parallel with the snath which may require slightly moving the scythe ring up or down along the snath to accommodate the desired angle. This is the basic assembly of the scythe and its adjustment to your body. As you mow, you may need to make subtle adjustments to fit your body, the way you move and the quality of the material to be mown.

7 *Adust the hafting angle step 2*

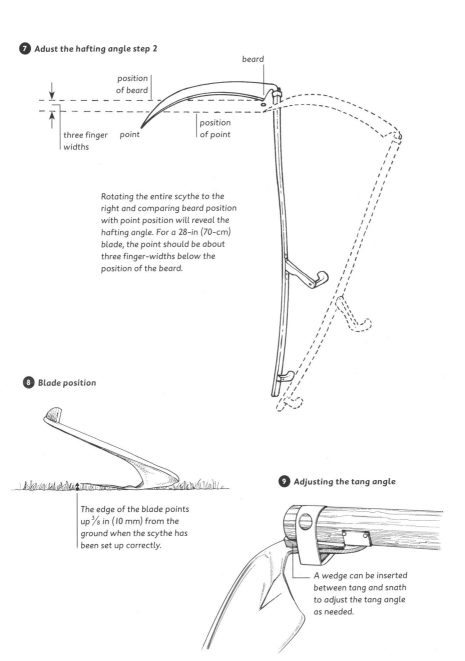

beard

position
of beard

three finger
widths

point

position
of point

Rotating the entire scythe to the
right and comparing beard position
with point position will reveal the
hafting angle. For a 28-in (70-cm)
blade, the point should be about
three finger-widths below the
position of the beard.

8 **Blade position**

The edge of the blade points
up ³⁄₈ in (10 mm) from the
ground when the scythe has
been set up correctly.

9 **Adjusting the tang angle**

A wedge can be inserted
between tang and snath
to adjust the tang angle
as needed.

Safety

A scythe, improperly handled or treated with too little respect, could maim or kill you or someone else. Fortunately, the converse is also true: a scythe, properly handled and respected, need never injure anyone. Here are a few guidelines for proper storage, handling and transport of the scythe.

The safest place for a scythe not in use, as long as everyone is aware of its location, is the ground, with the handles up and the blade edge in the grass, pointed down and away from passersby (do not place the blade edge on concrete or some other hard surface as it can damage the edge) 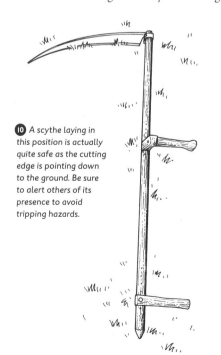. Anyone approaching an area with a scythe on the ground should be warned of its presence in case they trip over it, perhaps causing the blade to rise off the ground. If you are using

10 *A scythe laying in this position is actually quite safe as the cutting edge is pointing down to the ground. Be sure to alert others of its presence to avoid tripping hazards.*

11 *Use two hands to hold the scythe safely when it's not in use and you are stationary.*

a scythe and stop briefly to talk to someone, pick up the scythe, hold it vertically between the blade and right grip and place the non-blade end of the snath on the ground or on top of your foot. Hold the point with your left hand or point it away from yourself and anyone else **11**.

There is a popular folk image of mowers walking to the field with the snath resting on the shoulder, as if the scythe were a knapsack on a stick. This is extremely unsafe because of the high potential energy of the blade (it is being carried far above the ground and thus could fall a long distance, gaining speed as it falls), the difficulty in judging exactly where the blade is (it being behind you) and the possibility of your being less aware of it because it is out of sight.

Instead, use gravity to your advantage to find the safest carrying position. With your right hand down at your side, hold the scythe

12 *When walking with a scythe, hold it in your right hand at its natural balance point. The blade will naturally rotate away from your body.*

injure yourself or others, and it keeps the blade very much in your attention.

Hanging up the scythe is the safest way to store it while it is assembled. Nevertheless, be aware of the high potential energy of the blade. Whether your scythe is hung up at home for storage or temporarily in a tree, make sure that the point of the blade is hung higher than the tallest person who might come in contact with it and the lowest point of the scythe is out of the reach of children **13** . Avoid storing the scythe in direct sunlight, as heating the blade to above 212° F (100° C) will ruin the blade's tempering.

Two scythes can either be carried one in each hand, snath parallel to the ground as above, or with both in the right hand but with the blades staggered so that they don't touch each other, which could damage the cutting edge.

around the middle of the snath with the snath parallel to the ground. Now balance the snath on a finger or two in this position. Not only do you not have to apply effort to stabilize the scythe in this position, but the blade automatically points down and slightly out to the right. Twist the snath slightly to tip the blade up slightly more to the right, which ensures the blade will clear the ground as you walk **12** . Now the blade has a relatively low potential energy (being close to the ground, it could not fall far, nor could it pick up much speed) and it is right in front of you, so you know exactly where it is. The scythe can also be carried this way with the left hand, but extra effort is needed to twist the blade out to the left.

When there are a number of people present and you have to manoeuvre among them, hold the point of the blade with your left hand and the snath with your right. This makes it very unlikely that you could

13 *When hanging a scythe in a tree, be sure that the lowest part of the scythe is unreachable by children.*

The Mowing Stroke

When holding the scythe in the mowing position, the basic, neutral posture is legs slightly apart, knees free and slightly bent, right foot slightly ahead of the left, exactly halfway between the two grips on the snath. The attachment of the right grip is very near the right knee in the Upper Austrian snath, while the blade of the scythe makes contact with the ground in the area between the tang and the middle of the blade (adjust your hands as necessary to accomplish this) and the point of the blade points forward 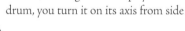 . Placing the right foot slightly ahead of the left causes you to face slightly to the left. The reason for this posture is that the blade of the scythe is already at the far right, so your mowing is biased to the right. Rotating slightly to the left corrects this bias and will also help keep your windrow of cut grass free from any uncut grass that may be to your left.

The scythe is drawn around the body in a semi-circle with the blade in constant contact with the ground, even on the return stroke **17** . Since the scythe is held with the hands, it can be tempting to focus effort on your hands and arms. To illustrate why this is not necessary, try playing a den-den daiko (Japanese pellet drum) or at least watch someone else doing it **15** . To play the drum, you turn it on its axis from side

14 The basic, "neutral" posture when holding the scythe in the mowing position.

to side. Tension at the attachment point of the strings sends the strings in the direction of the rest of the drum. Centrifugal force sends the beads on the ends of the strings upward and outward **16** . Without putting any effort directly into the strings and beads, they move and the drum sounds. So, pretend your body is this drum. Allow your hands, arms and shoulders to be completely free and spin at your spine – your axis – from side to side, observing your hands, arms and shoulders and imagining the scythe is in your hands. As you will discover, no effort whatsoever is required of your arms to produce the mowing stroke. The only effort required from the hands, arms and shoulders is to hold and stabilize the scythe.

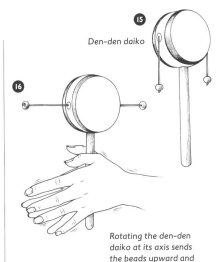

15

Den-den daiko

Rotating the den-den daiko at its axis sends the beads upward and outward.

17 The blade moves through the grass in a semi-circle.

18 Start of the mowing stroke.

19 Middle of the mowing stroke.

So now take the scythe in your hands and, as much as it may seem counter-intuitive at first, draw the scythe around your body in a semi-circle using both your core and your legs **18** **19** . The chine of the blade (the turned-up part perpendicular to the ground) shows the path the blade will take, so if you want to concentrate on something, make it

that. Keep the snath close to your body as you move it along and draw your left hand towards your spine as your upper body twists somewhat **20** . The stroke is completed when the point of the blade points backwards **21** . The shape of the blade, friction and gravity combine to release the cut grass from the blade on the return stroke,

21 Blade will point toward the rear at the end of the stroke.

20 End of the mowing stroke, left hand drawn in towards spine.

leaving a windrow of cut grass behind you to your left as you mow.

To get a good feel for the semi-circle that the scythe blade moves in, try mowing by only twisting the upper body from the spine. Watch the back of the blade as it moves in a semi-circle. Now oscillate the upper body from side to side by allowing your weight to shift from foot to foot (right foot for the mowing stroke, left foot for the return stroke) as you practise mowing and notice how the strength of your legs takes over much of the effort of mowing. And remember the cardinal rule – keep the scythe blade on the ground at all times while you are mowing!

Mowing

The mowing of grass results from a combination of the mowing stroke and advancing forward down the row. Just before every stroke (that is, during the return stroke) you take two tiny steps forward, advancing about 1½ in (4 cm). It is these 1½ in (4 cm) of grass (somewhat more for more experienced mowers and for longer blades) that are actually cut along each semi-circle made by each stroke.

Here's how to go about it. At the end of your stroke, just as you begin your return stroke (with the blade on the ground!), your weight will naturally be carried by your left leg, which frees up your right foot to take a small step forward. Then, just as your return stroke is coming to an end, take a small step forward with your left foot. You have now moved the whole mowing apparatus (your body, plus scythe) forward for the next stroke, which will cut the next 1½ in (4 cm) of grass in the row. As you get used to this, you will naturally slip into a waltz rhythm of 'stroke, step, step, stroke, step, step'. Pay attention to your breath as you mow, exhaling during the mowing stroke and inhaling during the return stroke.

As you begin to feel comfortable mowing, try playing around with the setup of the scythe to get an idea of what works better or worse for your body. Could the grips be set differently? What happens when you open up the hafting angle? And when you make it smaller? **22** .

To increase the width of the swathe that you mow, you may reach out to your right to get the blade further away from you as you end the return stroke. Do not attempt to increase the width of the swathe by

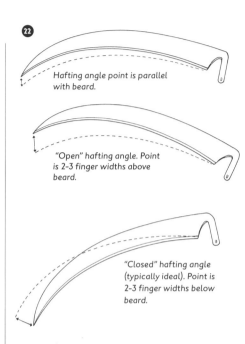

22

Hafting angle point is parallel with beard.

"Open" hafting angle. Point is 2-3 finger widths above beard.

"Closed" hafting angle (typically ideal). Point is 2-3 finger widths below beard.

increasing your reach on the left side, though, as this decreases overall efficiency and can potentially lead to knee soreness and/or injury. Some scythers recommend taking exaggerated steps to each side as you mow to increase the swathe width further, but my impression is that you lose efficiency in this way and I don't recommend it. I generally discourage anything that increases the amount of effort you have to put into mowing, even if it seems to increase your efficiency in the short term by increasing the width of the swathe. Having said that, go with what works for you.

There are many different kinds and lengths of scythe blades. Grass blades are usually 24–36 in (60–90 cm) in length. There are also shorter 20 in (50 cm), thicker bush blades for cutting out saplings in fields

Dripline Mulching *by* Michael Phillips

Orchard trees extend their feeder root system twice during the growing season. The 'spring root flush' kicks into gear immediately after blossom time, just as fruit begins to set. Nutrient uptake at this point is directed towards growing this year's crop, along with developing embryonic cells that will become next year's.

Feeder roots extend 1–2 in (2.5–5 cm) at most off the permanent root system of the tree. The majority of these lateral extensions are temporal – they have a particular job to do and are then shed. The ebb and flow of feeder-root growth is met with a similar response on the part of symbiotic mycorrhizal fungi. Their branching structure in effect broadens the roots' reach for nutrients just as the tree is capable of delivering more sugars to the mycorrhizal fungi in exchange.

Timing the first mowing of the orchard understorey to catch this rising tide creates favourable dynamics for the uptake of nutrients for growing fruit. Trees planted in a meadow-type ecosystem face competition from surrounding grasses and herbs. Scything down this sward within the drip line of each tree in the week or two when fruit has begun to set lays a carpet of mulch with textbook carbon-to-nitrogen ratio for fungi to thrive.

This 'fungal sweet spot' occurs when carbon levels of applied organic matter are 30–40 times higher than nitrogen. The timing here coincides with when farmers traditionally do a first cutting of hay. Seed heads are still immature, thus optimizing protein content for livestock, and the C:N ratio of such freshly cut grasses placed about fruit trees is perfect to prompt abundant fungal support without tying up nitrogen.

It's important that dripline mulch be laid down as full-length stalks, unchopped. Scything achieves this well. The growth suppression of surrounding plants gives the feeder roots of apples and other fruit a longer chance to work with fungal allies.

Down below, root shock to their plant competitors provides 'room in the humus' for tree feeder roots to access the greater share of nutrients in more complex forms. Infrequent mowing has an entirely different effect on grasses than does regular mowing. This first knockdown around the trees in late spring actually induces root pullback by ecosystem neighbours until those mowed plants recover thus allowing feeder roots and symbiotic mycorrhizal fungi to access soil nutrients that would have otherwise been taken up by neighbouring plants had they not been mowed. Fruit is well underway by that point, thanks to this biological mowing.

Michael Phillips is well known for helping people grow healthy fruit. See www.groworganicapples.com to learn more about his holistic approach to growing fruit. Michael's books include *The Apple Grower* and *The Holistic Orchard*.

or along fences, 30 cm (12 in) hand scythes and very long 43-in (110-cm) or more competitive-mowing blades. Try out as many different blades as you have access to, in order to experience what each of them feels like and can do. In general, shorter blades cut less grass (less advancing per stroke) but are easier to control. Longer blades allow you to take a deeper 'bite' with each stroke, but can be difficult to control at first and are very sensitive to small changes in the hafting angle. When mowing with a very short blade, like a bush blade, the arms can be used more to create the same motion of the blade in a much shorter stroke.

Now let's have a look at where to start mowing and in what pattern. Different people have different preferences, but I find it helpful to keep in mind the following principles:

1 Choose a pattern that requires the least amount of work.

2 Mow in such a way that the cut grass will fall through gravity alone and the cutting motion is supported by gravity (rather than in opposition to gravity).

3 Where grass is lodged (uncut, but lying on the ground), cut into the bend in the grass from behind. When mowing from the other side, the edge of the scythe blade is likely to glide up over the lodged blades of grass, rather than cut into them.

4 Mow hillsides diagonally up to the left, from bottom to top, to avoid the danger of slipping or falling on to the blade and to use gravity to your advantage in laying down cut grass.

5 See to it that the windrows lie in such a way as to be easily accessible with the methods you will use to bring the harvest in (cart, baler, hay rack, and so forth). Keep in mind the height and width of equipment and whether it can fit between trees or other potential obstacles.

CHALLENGING MOWING SITUATIONS
When you are preparing to tackle a flat meadow that is regularly mowed and therefore contains no saplings, there is nothing more to it than thinking through the ideal pattern based on shape, loading the finished product, and mowing as described above. However, it's likely that you may be faced instead with a few typical challenges.

Some meadows contain trees or shrubs, and you may even wish to mow an orchard. The goal here is to mow in a way that will not damage the trees or your scythe, while still mowing all the way up to the trunks, keeping the grass accessible and maintaining a comfortable action. To achieve this, mow towards the tree until you no longer feel confident that the next sweep of your scythe will miss it. Then, with short strokes, using mainly your arms and the half of the blade that includes the point, mow the rest of the way to the trunk. When you reach it, place the chine of the scythe blade (the 'back' of the blade) near the point against the trunk **23** and mow away from the trunk with a short, quick stroke **24**. Move around the trunk mowing in this way, gently placing the chine of the blade near the point against the base of the tree and cutting away, so that when you have mowed all the way around, the base of the tree is free of uncut grass.

23 *Gently touching the tree with the chine at the point protects the tree...*

24 *...and sets you up to make a short stroke away from the tree.*

25 *Free the first windrow from standing grass by mowing back in the other direction.*

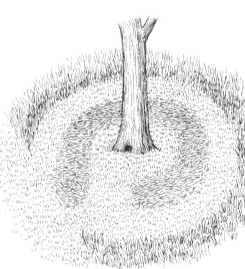

26 *A successfully mowed-out tree.*

Now you have cut grass lying among uncut grass, except where you approached the tree. To free the circular windrow you've just cut from the uncut meadow, mow your way back the other way around to the beginning, starting on the outside of the circular windrow. Cut a swathe so that your strokes end underneath the circular windrow, perhaps pushing the windrow back towards the tree a bit **25** . When you have returned to where you started with the tree, there will be a dense windrow of cut grass around and away from the tree and free of the uncut meadow **26** .

Where meadows border paved or gravel roads, mow in a pattern that prevents the edge of the scythe blade coming into contact with their surface. Instead of mowing one

27 *Mow a steep slope from the bottom, reaching to the right to start the mowing stroke as high as possible.*

28 *The stroke finishes in a more or less neutral position.*

wide swathe along the edge and risking damage to the blade, mow at right angles to the road at the edge and pay attention to the chine of the blade. Use this technique also for stream beds or any other such dangerous elements bordering the meadow.

When you are mowing steep hills, plan your path so that you are never mowing directly uphill. The efficient windrowing and release of grass by the scythe blade depends on gravity, and that is something that should always be used to your advantage while mowing (this will quickly become clear to you if you try to defy gravity as you will tire very quickly). Mow from the bottom of the hill up, diagonally if possible, or if the hill is too steep mow horizontally across it making a half swathe from your right to the middle as shown in the illustrations **27** **28** .

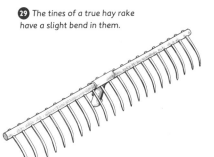

29 The tines of a true hay rake have a slight bend in them.

Hay and wet, freshly cut grass will often get stuck in the tines. Press the tines against the ground for the first 6 in (15 cm) as you move the head of the rake away from you to rake more grass. The increased friction causes the grass to free itself from the rake.

RAKING Though much of the process of raking grass and hay is obvious, there are a few extra wrinkles that will save you time, effort and frustration.

True hay rakes are made with tines that are not only bent back toward the raker from the base, but also have a bend in the middle **29**.

This allows the tines to glide across the ground while picking up hay instead of getting caught in the ground and disturbing the soil, causing you extra effort. As the head of the rake nears your body, raise the handle of the rake until it is near vertical when the rake head is at your feet **30**.

CLEANING AND CARE OF YOUR SCYTHE Wash and dry the blade of the scythe after every mowing to remove plant material, sap and soil. For winter storage, wash the blade and oil it with food-grade oil or WD40. Motor oil (including synthetics) and chain saw oil are not appropriate as the former causes a host of environmental problems and the latter quickly becomes resinous.

30 Making the handle more vertical as you pull the head of the rake towards you keeps hay on the rake without the rake getting caught on the ground.

Allow the twisting of your torso with your core
muscles to be the source of power as you mow.

CHAPTER 3 GETTING THE BEST FROM YOUR BODY

In many ways, the things we do in our lives are different kinds of dances. When we go running, we do a particular dance; when we sit down in a chair, we do another, and so on. Mowing with a scythe is about finding a way of dancing with the scythe in your hands so that in the end there's a pile of cut grass behind you and you feel as if you've hardly done anything.

Engaging in a new activity such as mowing with the scythe can be an opportunity to let go of arbitrary habits and start afresh in the way you use your body. There are several established paths for doing this, including the Alexander Technique, the Feldenkrais Method and the Gokhale Method. In the modern world, especially in the West with our sedentary and high-stress lifestyles, our bodies take on all kinds of seemingly arbitrary habits that are not beneficial to our well-being. And, as a Guitar Craft aphorism states, 'It is difficult to exaggerate the power of habit.'

31 *Lengthening the spine through the crown of the skull as chin rests on index finger.*

32 *Support your legs with the minimum effort required to prevent them falling inward or outward.*

Alexander Technique

I am not an Alexander Technique teacher, but I took lessons for a while and I would like to share here the aspects of it that helped my mowing immensely. First, the concept of inhibition, a word that has its own special meaning in the context of the Alexander Technique. Our thoughts can trigger a chain reaction of muscle tensions and habits that acts so fast as to be nearly imperceptible. Therefore, the moment you think, 'I'm going to mow some grass,' or 'I'm going to swing the scythe,' your body fires off a series of subtle motions and tensions based on past experiences. Inhibition, in the Alexander Technique world, means actively saying no to this 'habit energy'. This means more than just doing nothing and makes it possible to say yes to doing something from a neutral place.

Another key Alexander Technique concept is the lengthening of the spine. This is different from standing, sitting up straight, or holding any kind of posture. It is about your spine continually being engaged in the dynamic process of lengthening lead by the crown of your skull no matter what you are doing – whether sitting, standing, mowing or whatever – so that the muscles that connect your spine with your skull (the sub-occipitals) can completely relax.

Counter-intuitive as it may seem, your chin will tend to tuck in towards your throat as your spine lengthens, so that you can rest your chin on your index finger when you hold your thumb and middle finger against your clavicle (collarbone). In fact, pushing up on your clavicle with your right hand in this position while pushing down on your belly button with your other thumb is the technique used in Chi Running for lengthening the spine **31** .

A lengthened spine is not a posture to hold but a dynamic process to engage in. As you mow, lengthen the spine while doing as little as possible with your arms and legs. Allow the twisting of your torso with your core muscles to be the source of power as you mow.

Finally, constructive rest is a way of releasing your body from the demands of gravity to help you use it in the right way and release excess tension. While it is best to learn this from an Alexander teacher, here is a basic description. Lie on your back on a firm surface with your knees elevated and your head supported on a few books – your chin should be lower than your forehead but not pressed into your throat **32** . Support

Primary directions

- I allow the muscles of my neck to be free from tension
- As I allow my whole head to release up and off the top of my spine
- So that my whole spinal column lengthens and my whole back lengthens and widens
- I allow my hips, ribs and shoulders to widen
- As my elbows free one away from the other and my knees free up towards the ceiling
- I allow my feet to release towards the floor and the palms of my hands to rest on my lower ribs.

Additional directions

- Allow your breath to flow naturally in and out of your body. Do not force inhalation or exhalation, but rather allow the natural movement of your breath to take place.
- You may include in your directions an overall yielding of the weight of yourself to the floor, a quieting of excessive nervous and muscular activity, and an alertness of your senses.

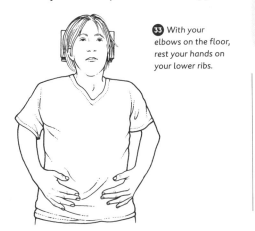

33 With your elbows on the floor, rest your hands on your lower ribs.

your knees in the air with the minimum effort required to prevent them falling away from or towards each other. With your elbows on the floor, rest the palms of your hands on your lower ribs **33** . Now direct your body as advised by Alexander Technique teacher Laurel Podulke-Smith in her article 'Constructive Rest' (see panel above).

The ideal is to do constructive rest every day for 15–20 minutes. I do it instead on an as-needed basis, when I realize that muscles are starting to get overly tense (usually in my neck and shoulders). If I'm mowing a large patch that may take several hours or even all day, I may do constructive rest every hour or so. I am consistently amazed at how well it helps me to recover and get back into lengthening my spine.

Something you may notice when you first start using your body in this way is that everything feels 'wrong'. This is one of the tricks that bad habits in the use of the body play on us – they start to feel normal. When you start to use your body in the right way it will feel wrong or awkward until your muscles and brain readjust to different movements. This can be confusing and discouraging at first, but teachers of various techniques of the use of the self can help you through the process.

One final concept that is always in the back of my mind when I mow is expressed in the Guitar Craft aphorism 'Honour necessity, honour sufficiency.' In other words, honour necessity by putting forth the effort that is required and nothing less; honour sufficiency by putting forth the effort that is required and nothing more.

Meditation

For me, meditation is a technique that keeps my stress level at a minimum, promotes bodily awareness and increases focus, and as such it can help with mowing. Practised daily over a period of years, meditation actually alters your brain, creating new neural networks. The more you meditate, the more deeply these new networks establish themselves and the more you experience the effects of meditation in your day-to-day life even while you are not meditating.

I have found that stress is perhaps the main reason for lapsing into poor technique while mowing. The more my mind is wandering and I am not present with the task at hand, the more likely I am to slip into old habits: unnecessary tensions, muscles taking on tasks for which they weren't designed, ultimately using much more energy than is necessary. This quickly leads to fatigue, frustration and quitting early. Meditation tends to prevent this cascade of ineffectiveness from starting in the first place.

When you meditate, you often become aware of unnecessary tensions that you are holding in your body. As the mindfulness that you experience during meditation increasingly infiltrates your daily life, you will become increasingly aware of your body and stresses that you can let go of in the various tasks you perform, including mowing with the scythe.

Finally, the more you are able to focus on the task at hand, the more effective you will be. An improved state of mindfulness helps

Meditation Exercise

My own personal meditation practice is a combination of the transcendental meditation technique and the Benson-Henry Protocol, which is itself a generic version of transcendental meditation.

* I start by sitting in a quiet, comfortable place where I will not be disturbed, such as a chair in my bedroom. If necessary, I will turn on a fan for white noise to drown out barking dogs or what have you.

* I then close my eyes and take about a minute to progressively relax my muscles starting from my toes and going all the way up to the top of my skull.

* At this point I begin repeating my mantra to myself in my head while keeping my eyes closed. When you take a transcendental meditation class, you receive a personalized mantra. As it turns out, a personalized mantra is no more or less effective than any word or phrase with neutral or positive connotations, such as 'one' or 'peace'.

* Assume a passive attitude throughout your meditation as best you can. It's not about clearing your mind of thoughts. Thoughts are inevitable. That's what the brain does; it thinks. Meditation is about engaging in the process of returning to your focus (a mantra, your breath, an image).

* When your mind wanders, as it inevitably will, and you notice it, just think, 'Oh well,' and return to your focus. You will probably do this several times each time you meditate.

In transcendental meditation, I was taught to meditate twice a day for 20 minutes, so I usually do that. The Benson-Henry Protocol recommends 12-15 minutes at least once a day. I meditate once before breakfast to start the day and once in the late afternoon. I never meditate right after eating; it just doesn't work well. Make a commitment to meditating at least once a day for 30 days. By then, it will have become part of your routine.

you to make better decisions such as what pattern to mow a given patch in, and gives you a better feel for when to hone and the prioritizing of things that make for better mowing (peening, getting up early to take advantage of morning dew and so on).

There are many different kinds of meditation, a number of which have nothing to do with religion except that the techniques often originated in religious traditions. Secular meditation techniques include the Benson-Henry Protocol, transcendental meditation (TM), which I practise, mindfulness-based stress reduction (MBSR) and progressive muscle relaxation, among others.

CHAPTER 4 GETTING THE BEST FROM YOUR SCYTHE

Scythes are made so that the middle of the rear of the blade rests on the ground for the entire stroke. A popular misconception is that the scythe blade is lifted while swinging and then the ground is hacked at from above, with grass only being cut at the one spot where the blade touches the ground before it bounces back up again. This is entirely wrong.

Any lifting of the blade from the ground is not only wasted effort but also reduces the amount of grass that is cut per stroke, thus further increasing the overall energy required to mow a given area of grass.

The scythe blade is kept on the ground and moved through the grass in a semi-circle. If the hafting angle – that is, the angle of the blade to the snath that is established at the point of attachment – were set so that the cutting edge of the blade were perpendicular to the semi-circle the scythe is being moved in, it would simply lay the grass down flat, no matter how sharp the edge. Imagine trying to cut a loaf of spongy yeasted bread with a serrated bread knife by placing the edge on top of the loaf and just pressing straight down. It might cut a bit at the top of the loaf, but otherwise the whole loaf would just be pinched down against the cutting surface. To cut the bread, the serrated edge needs to glide back and forth across the loaf. To cut grass, the hafting angle needs to be set so that the blade can bite into the grass, then glide through and on to the next stroke.

34 The middle of the rear of the scythe blade rests on the ground for the entire stroke.

Primary zone of contact of blade with the ground

Optimizing the Hafting Angle

When the hafting angle is set so that the blade moves through the grass perfectly parallel to the cutting semi-circle, the only grass that will be cut with each stroke is the amount found in the ground in the width of the blade itself. The cut is caused by the differential in the width of the blade from the point to the beard. The closer the tang angle is to parallel with the cutting semi-circle, the easier it is to mow, but the less grass is cut with each stroke. The more open the hafting angle is, the more grass can theoretically be cut with each stroke, but the more difficult it is to move the blade through the grass and the more likely it is that a given blade of grass will not be cut but laid down. So, you're looking for a happy medium between being able to take deeper "bites" out of the meadow with each stroke than with a blade set perfectly parallel to the mowing semi-circle, yet not opening up the angle so much that each stroke becomes too strenuous. The exact hafting angle becomes more and more important the longer the blade is, since the point of a longer blade displaces more from the cutting semi-circle than a shorter blade at the same angle.

As you mow, try different hafting angles. Mow for a minute with the point 4–6 fingers below the beard. Switch to 2–3 fingers below the beard, then with the point even with the beard, then switch to 2–3 fingers above. Hone between each change of angle, so you can be sure that any difference you feel is not due to changes in the sharpness of the scythe. Are you able to mow more effectively and efficiently in the new position? Or less?

The Meeting of Scythe and Grass

When you peel a carrot, the blade of the peeler bites into the carrot through a combination of pressure on the blade and the resistance given by the hand holding the carrot. A similar kind of tension is created between the shape of the scythe blade – with the edge slightly curving up from the ground when the blade is in the cutting position – and the blade of grass rooted in the soil.

The moving edge of the scythe blade makes contact with an anchored, ideally wet (water's surface tension increases friction) blade of grass, causing the grass to be pulled taut and resistant as the blade's edge penetrates the grass. Since the anchoring effect of the roots is far stronger than the pressure exerted on the grass by the razor-sharp blade, the grass is cut rather than uprooted.

This is how it happens ideally; variables are the motion of the scythe, the hafting angle, the shape and sharpness of the blade and the moisture level, texture, position and length of the blade of grass. When all these things are in harmony with each other, mowing proceeds with an ease that never ceases to amaze even experienced mowers.

CHAPTER 5 BLADE CARE: HONING TO PERFECTION

The blade of the scythe cuts through hundreds of blades of grass with each stroke and eventually the ultra-fine outer edge becomes dulled enough for you to notice an increase in the effort required to mow, which usually manifests itself in increased use of the arms and shoulders. Though the blade is still sharp enough to easily cause injury, it needs to be brought back to razor-sharpness in order for that hot-knife-through-butter ease of mowing to return.

The way to sharpen a scythe is to scrape a whetstone across the edge of the blade to smooth out uneven, dulled edges and restore its sharpness – a process known as honing.

When to Hone

How can you tell how often you need to hone while mowing? The short answer is that you hone every time you notice that it is getting harder to mow, so that simply using your body is no longer enough; your arms and shoulders are also required to execute the mowing stroke. This will be about every 5–10 minutes, depending on your mowing rate, the coarseness of the material being mowed and how recently the scythe was peened. Apart from honing while mowing, you also need to hone the scythe before and after peening.

It can be tempting to keep your head down and plough through the mowing, pausing as little as possible, in the mistaken belief that repeated honing will prolong the mowing and won't make it much easier. In my experience, waiting too long to hone will not only extend the time it takes to mow the same parcel of land and reduce the quality of the cut, but will also lead to frustration and maybe even injury, which will decrease your enjoyment of mowing and probably, sooner or later, lead to you find some other way to mow. Honing too infrequently leads to a vicious cycle of inefficiency and frustration. Listen to your body and hone as often as you need to maintain pleasant and efficient mowing. Pausing to hone will bring greater ease to your mowing.

Using the Right Whetstone

Hard natural whetstones remove almost no material when whetting but instead restore the shape of the edge of a blade which has been slightly deformed by coming in contact with small rocks or woody stems while mowing. Use on blades peened maximally thin for mowing tender grass.

Soft natural whetstones act abrasively, but only minimally, and help to reshape a slightly deformed blade edge by removing tiny amounts of material from the edge to restore its smoothness. Use on blades peened not quite to maximum thinness for mowing slightly tougher and/or slightly drier grass.

Fine-grit artificial whetstones are only slightly more abrasive than soft natural whetstones. Use on blades peened for mowing slightly coarser grass.

Medium-grit artificial whetstones are quite abrasive and remove a fair amount of material from the edge of the blade. Use on bush blades or grass blades peened for harvesting small grains, nettles or other strong-stemmed plants.

Coarse-grit artificial whetstones are the most abrasive, capable of removing the most material from the edge of the blade. Use on bush blades.

Whetstones, Natural and Artificial

Whetstones are either cut from natural stone or manufactured from various resins and abrasives. Natural whetstones are always used wet (they do not hone when dry) and are therefore carried in a holder with water while mowing, except for those made from new red sandstone, which can be used dry. Artificial whetstones will hone when dry, however using them wet is generally better as it contributes to a longer life for both whetstone and blade.

Natural whetstones are best for general grass mowing as they have a finer grit than artificial stones and therefore remove less material from the blade's edge, allowing for a finer, sharper edge, which is needed for mowing fine, succulent grass. Choose a hard slate or granite whetstone for fine, tender grass; for more brittle, 'woodier' grasses and meadow plants, use one made of soft slate or sandstone.

Artificial whetstones are suited to a first rough honing of a grass blade that has not been peened for a long time (to be immediately followed by a finer honing with a natural stone) or for thicker, harder bush blades that are not sharpened to such a thin cutting edge and where removing more material during honing is appropriate. Do not use an artificial whetstone on a well-peened grass blade, as this will remove too much material, ruin the edge and cause you to have to re-peen the scythe. Artificial whetstones are available in fine, middle and coarse grits, as well as two-sided stones, with one fine side and one rough side.

Hone as often as required to maintain pleasant, efficient mowing.

Honing Technique

35 *Before honing, clean plant debris from the blade by wiping from beard to point with long, cut grass folded over the chine.*

Honing methods vary from region to region and are an individual choice too. Some people place the heel of the blade on their knee with the point oriented upwards; others shove the snath under an arm, with the blade pointing to the ground; still others rest the snath on their upper leg with the blade pointed upwards. Here I shall describe the Austrian style of honing, which seems to me the easiest and safest.

What is common to all honing techniques is to first clean the blade **35** . A dirty blade

with plant debris, plant sap and soil stuck to it will not hone evenly along its length and could even damage the blade by causing uneven sharpness, potentially leading to warpage or deep serrations. Also, getting too much plant sap or soil on the whetstone can make it dirty and greasy, causing it to no longer hone effectively; if it does occur, soak the whetstone in vinegar and water for 12 hours to dissolve grease and dirt.

To clean the blade, hold the scythe upright, with the butt end of the snath on the ground

36 *Hold the blade by the chine while honing.*

or on top of your foot and the back of the blade in your left hand. With your right hand, drape a handful of freshly mown grass over the back of the blade so that it covers the top and underside. Squeezing as you go (but not touching the blade edge), wipe grass and dirt from the blade, and then you are ready to hone.

There are three important components of honing: how you hold the scythe, how you hold the whetstone and how you move the whetstone along the blade.

Hold the snath upright so that the blade is in the air (not on the ground) and pointing to the left. The butt end of the snath can be on the ground or, to keep it clean and dry, on top of your right foot. Hold the blade by its upturned chine (not the underside that glides across the ground) **36** .

How you handle the whetstone is crucial for your safety. Hold it near the bottom of the stone with your thumb tucked underneath your index finger **37** . Tucking in your thumb is essential to keep it away from the

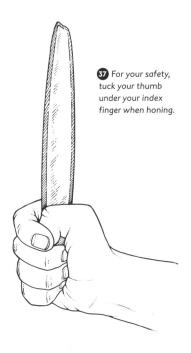

37 *For your safety, tuck your thumb under your index finger when honing.*

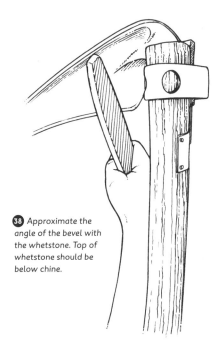

38 *Approximate the angle of the bevel with the whetstone. Top of whetstone should be below chine.*

edge of the blade; neglecting this detail can lead to a major injury of your hand.

Honing is a sharpening and smoothing of the edge of the scythe blade, not a filing off of blade deformations. It is achieved by gliding the whetstone along the edge with moderate pressure. This is most safely and easily done with several short strokes, alternating from the underside to the top side of the blade (not one long stroke on each side), from beard to point. The reason for honing in this direction is that, at a microscopic level, the edge is not smooth but serrated, like a saw. Having these 'teeth' as small as possible and oriented towards the point ('against' the grass) makes for better cutting.

For your safety, perform each stroke by moving the whetstone not only along the

blade's edge but also away (down) from it at the same time **38** **39** . This way, as you work your way down the edge toward the point, each stroke always leads you away from the edge, not along it, and you need only be sure that your hand is safely away from the edge of the blade at the beginning of each stroke. If the top of the whetstone is touching the chine of the blade, you are starting too high in that your hand is probably too close to the edge for safety and the whetstone will not be lying on the edge at an appropriate angle.

It is crucial that you hold the whetstone at an angle that approximates the shape of the edge. The blade is single bevelled, so the whetstone should be parallel to the blade along the underside and at a slight angle (the angle of the bevel) along the topside. Slowly

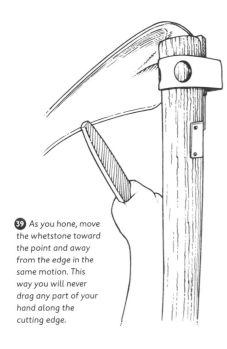

39 As you hone, move the whetstone toward the point and away from the edge in the same motion. This way you will never drag any part of your hand along the cutting edge.

work your way from beard to point in short strokes, shifting the position you hold the blade's chine with your left hand as needed to provide support. By proceeding in this way, every spot along the edge will have been touched by the whetstone a few times once you've reached the point. Pay close attention to the angle of the whetstone at the point, since the blade is so narrow there that it can be difficult to approximate the angle of the bevel. If mowing is not significantly easier, hone again and apply a bit more pressure.

Keep your whetstone wet and with you while you mow by putting it in a water-filled holder on your belt. If your water is particularly hard and limescale is showing up on your whetstone, add some vinegar to the water.

Each stroke of the whetstone should lead away from the edge while moving along it.

CHAPTER 6 **BLADE CARE: THE PEENING PROCESS**

Through mowing and honing, the edge of the blade slowly wears away. When you are no longer able to get it as sharp as you would like and it doesn't hold its sharpness for long, it is time to peen. Peening is the rejuvenating of the cutting edge by cold hammering it against an anvil to draw more material to the edge and harden it. How often you will need to do this depends on the quality of the material you have been mowing since the last peening – woody, coarse plants or soft, succulent grass. The blade will certainly require peening after 10–12 hours of mowing, but you may ultimately find it easier to do a faster (yet still thorough), softer peening after every 2–5 hours of mowing. Peening more frequently means each session is quicker and easier, taking 10-15 minutes depending on the length of the blade.

ake peening a regular part of your mowing routine and it will no longer seem like an extra task you have to do. Just go out and mow for a couple of hours in the morning while the dew is still on the grass, then bring the scythe back in and peen it for 15 minutes before putting it away.

It is obvious that it is crucial to know how to mow with the scythe for it to be of much use to you. What is perhaps less obvious is how important it is to keep the scythe sharp. Efficient, effective mowing with the scythe is a combination of a smooth, gentle and correct mowing technique, a properly adjusted snath and an absolutely razor-sharp blade. If you are not able to keep the blade sharp yourself and no one else in your area can do this, the effortlessness of mowing with the scythe will quickly disappear and mowing will turn into an unpleasant chore that you will neglect or maybe suffer injury from, no matter how good your mowing technique is.

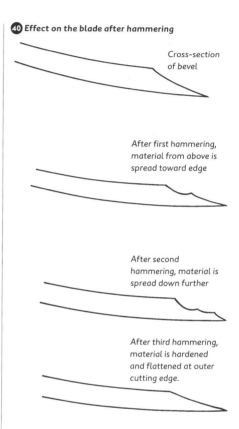

40 *Effect on the blade after hammering*

Cross-section of bevel

After first hammering, material from above is spread toward edge

After second hammering, material is spread down further

After third hammering, material is hardened and flattened at outer cutting edge.

When to Peen

At a certain point, as the material of the blade wears away through mowing and honing, the only way to restore sharpness to the edge of the blade is through peening. This is a way of moving material down from the body of the blade into the edge and shaping and hardening it for further use, achieved by the cold hammering of the blade with a hammer against an anvil. You hammer along the length of the edge three times, once to bring material down, a second time to bring it down somewhat further and form

the bevel and a third time to form the razor-sharp cutting edge **40** . Cold hammering compresses the molecular structure of the materials of the blade, which means that peening hardens the edge of the blade. A good cutting edge should be sufficiently thin and sharp, yet not wear away too quickly and be easy to hone with a whetstone.

Originally, scythes were exclusively made by forging, but today they are also made by stamping or punching. Forged scythes are generally of much higher quality than stamped scythes in that they are lighter, thinner, less brittle and can be made sharper. They are also more expensive than stamped scythes.

Ideally, scythe blades are made of high-carbon steel (0.7–0.8 per cent being ideal) and not ultra-high-carbon steel (1 per cent carbon content or more). The higher the carbon content of the steel, the harder and more brittle it is. Stamped scythes are often thick and made with ultra-high-carbon steel, making them pretty much impossible to peen without cracking. An ideal scythe blade has a sharp cutting edge, mows well with little effort and holds its sharpness long. The quality of mowing possible with a scythe depends in large part on the hardness of the steel, the quality of the cutting edge and the shape of the blade. If the blade is too soft, the edge will be worn away quickly; if it is too hard, peening and honing will be difficult. A blade that holds its sharpness well means longer breaks between honing and therefore less overall honing.

Preparing the Blade

Peening works best when the blade's edge is clean, smooth and still somewhat sharp, free of warpage and nicks and has a good, normally curved form. So, before peening, hone with a coarse whetstone, file nicks and any parts of the edge that have bent up so that the entire edge is smooth and sand with a sanding sponge, sandpaper or an angle grinder (with sanding wheel). When sanding with an angle grinder, do it in short pulses to avoid heating the blade to above 212° F (100° C), as this would ruin the blade's tempering.

Hammers, Anvils and Jigs

There are three widely available techniques for peening: with a narrow anvil and flat-faced hammer; with a flat (wide) anvil and cross peen (narrow) hammer; and with a peening jig. When peening with a narrow anvil (Styrian-style peening), you have to be very careful about where you place the blade on the anvil, but not as careful about where exactly the hammer strikes. If you are peening with a flat anvil (Upper Austrian-style peening), the opposite applies: you need not be as careful about where the blade is on the anvil, but your hammer strikes have to be pretty exact. When peening with a jig, you do not need to be nearly as careful about how you proceed, but results are less satisfactory then when peening with hammer and anvil, plus you are dependent on a piece of specialized equipment, so I never use a jig.

Ultimately, the details of exactly how you peen are less important than you being able to peen in a way that is not overly strenuous for your body and results in a sharp, durable, smooth cutting edge that is free of 'teeth' and warpage. I prefer Styrian-style, narrow-anvil peening as I find it relatively easy to slowly advance the blade down the narrow anvil, paying close attention to exactly how I position the blade. With hammering, I only need to ensure that I am hitting vertically and hard enough. So here I shall describe peening in detail in the Styrian style.

Getting Set Up

Peening anvils are embedded in some sort of support to absorb the impact of the hammer and allow the person peening to work comfortably. A log a bit longer than the measurement from the bottom of your foot to just above your knee or a round cut out of a thick log are cheap, accessible options. A stone block, about 30 in (76 cm) high and around 2 ft (61 cm) long can also be used. Cut a wedge-shaped hole of about 1½ in (4 cm) in diameter in the stone with a hammer and chisel and use branch cuttings (ideally from willow) to wedge the anvil in the hole. Alternatively, pound your anvil into the top of your log with a rubber or wooden mallet or use your peening hammer with a piece of wood in between the hammer and anvil so as to not damage the anvil **41** .

Sit on a chair or log that allows your legs to be at a 90-degree angle **42** . Hold the blade by the back with your left hand and stabilize your left hand and the blade with your right leg.

The time it takes to peen a scythe blade depends on the quality of the metal, how long ago the previous peening was, the length of the blade and the ability of the person doing the peening. If you are peening a 24-in (60-cm) blade that was peened only a few days ago and has no damage and you are confident and efficient at peening, you may only need 10 minutes. On the other hand, if you have a 37-in (90-cm) blade that hasn't been peened for a long time and has a few dents in it, you may need to dedicate an hour or more to the task.

41 Pound anvil into log with a rubber mallet or use a piece of wood when pounding in with an iron hammer as here.

42 Basic posture while peening, with blade being held in place with left hand and resting on leg.

How To Peen

When hammering the blade the first time, the blade is positioned on the anvil so that it overlaps the anvil's peak by the amount you want to 'bite off' the blade – normally about 4mm, which is the width of the bevel **44**. Honing and sanding the edge gives it a sort of matt finish. When you start to hammer the blade, it shows up as a glossy line that contrasts with the matt edge and extends down the edge as you hammer along it. Use this glossy line to ensure that you are hammering where you want to.

Peening hammers and anvils are slightly rounded in every direction so that each hit directly impresses upon only one small point along the edge of the blade. Any errant blow thus does not lead to widespread damage.

Place the blade face down on the anvil with the beard in the middle, overlapping the top of the anvil towards your body by about 4mm and with the edge parallel to the ground. Hold the blade at the back with your left hand **43**. Begin hammering at the beard and slowly creep the blade along the top of the anvil from left to right as you advance towards the point. Ensure that you always hit the blade with the hammer at 90 degrees at the point of impact. The edge of the blade should not get nearer to or farther from your body as you proceed.

The idea is to hit the blade hard enough to make a shiny mark on it. The impact needs to be hard enough to 'bite off' some of the material of the scythe from above and shift it down ever so slightly, yet it must be soft enough not to cause cracking and consistent enough along the length of the blade not to cause warpage. It is better to do

43 Holding the blade just right on the anvil is the key to accurate peening.

it lightly at first. If you try out the scythe and sense that it is not much sharper, you will know that you need to peen again and hit harder.

When you've completed the first 'row' of hammering, which will appear as a continuous line across the blade, return to the beard and do it again, this time from a position that is closer to the very edge of the blade **45** . Keep the edge just beyond the peak of the anvil. This spreads the material you've bitten off with the first hammering down to the edge. When the second row is completed, hammer the blade one more time, this time at the very edge. Have the edge of the blade exactly at the peak of the anvil **46** . This last hammering hardens the material at the very edge for maximum sharpness and durability.

When you have finished peening, give the blade's edge the 'fingernail test', pressing up against the edge from the underside of the blade. A blade sharp enough for cutting even the finest of grasses will give a bit as you push up against it. This will probably be your standard sharpness for making hay. Another test for sharpness is to grip the body of the blade with your thumb on top and index or middle finger on the bottom. Slide your finger towards the edge, noting the thickness of the blade. An optimally peened blade should feel as if it goes from full thickness to seemingly no thickness over the last ⅛ in (4 mm) of metal that make up the bevel and cutting edge of the blade. For mowing coarser material such as nettles or small grains, a blade this sharp will not be strong enough and you will damage it sooner or later (probably sooner). Instead, peen so that the edge is a bit narrower than it would

otherwise be and does not give when pressing up with a fingernail. Alternatively, use a grass blade that would otherwise be in need of peening and hone it with a coarse artificial whetstone.

For your first attempt at peening, use a practice blade or a piece of sheet metal if possible, so you can get a feel for what needs to happen before starting the blade(s) you use to mow. Softer metals bend more easily, harder metals require a harder hit, brittle metals crack more easily – you need to slowly learn how to work with these various qualities.

Keep peening tools free of rust, nicks and dents. Store them in the driest conditions possible, occasionally clean and polish the striking surfaces of the hammer and anvil with steel wool and coat them with food-grade oil at the end of the mowing season. Use your scythe-peening tools only for this purpose. Even small damage to the striking surface of the hammer or anvil can cause problems with peening and potentially damage the scythe.

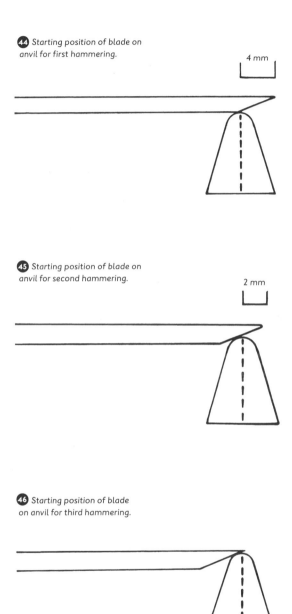

44 *Starting position of blade on anvil for first hammering.*

4 mm

45 *Starting position of blade on anvil for second hammering.*

2 mm

46 *Starting position of blade on anvil for third hammering.*

Troubleshooting

Your first attempts at peening will probably not be entirely successful and it is not always easy to know why, so here is a guide to common problems:

+ A curled or bowed edge is the result of not holding the blade level as you peen. A blade with such an edge does not cut grass effectively, which is bad enough, but instead lays the grass down, which makes it harder to mow – even with a blade that has a properly bevelled edge 47 .

+ A flat edge is caused by using an anvil with a hitting surface that is not rounded in all directions. This causes a small 'step' to form near the edge of the blade. A flat edge is more easily damaged by coarse plants than a bevelled edge, and is no longer effective because the whetstone is prevented from touching the entire edge by the 'step' 47 .

+ A deeply serrated edge is the result of moving the blade along too quickly and missing spots along the edge, meaning there are spots where the blade materials were stretched and other spots where they were not. Such toothed edges do not cut as well, nor do they move smoothly through the grass, resulting in increased effort in mowing and more uncut blades of grass left behind 48 .

+ A warped (wavy) edge comes from hitting too hard, which spreads the materials of the blade out too far 49 . The more wavy the edge, the less effective both honing and mowing will be. Wavy edges are next to impossible to repair as they release the

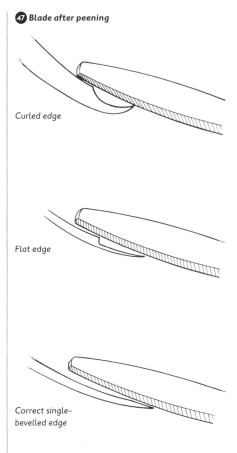

47 Blade after peening

Curled edge

Flat edge

Correct single-bevelled edge

original tension that was created in the blade during the forging process. To avoid creating a wavy edge, do not stretch the materials of the blade more than about 1 mm. Waves start as tiny hairline cracks; ideally they should not appear at all, but if they do start to form, they are a warning that you should not hit so hard.

start of bevel

48 *Deep serrations caused by spaces between hammer hits.*

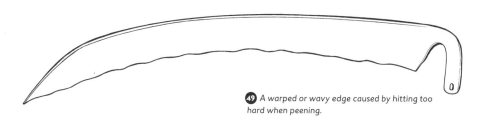

49 *A warped or wavy edge caused by hitting too hard when peening.*

Different Blades and Edges for Different Jobs

The coarser and woodier the plants that you want to mow, the shorter, sturdier and thicker the scythe blade and its cutting edge will need to be. Conversely, the softer, more succulent and shorter the material you want to mow (and the smoother the surface of the soil), the longer the blade can be and the sharper and thinner you can peen the edge.

+ Mowing the lawn requires the sharpest, thinnest edge you can manage because you will probably be mowing fairly short grass, which will not cut as easily. Allow your lawn to grow to the maximum length you feel comfortable with for the most effective mowing result. The number of obstacles such as paths and lawn ornaments and the smoothness of the soil surface will largely influence the length of blade that is practical to use.

+ Hay-making is another task requiring a maximally sharp and thin edge. The only caveat is if there are coarser plants mixed in with the grasses and clovers of the hay field, you may wish to make the edge slightly more robust than otherwise. Use the longest blade appropriate to your skill level and soil surface smoothness for maximum efficiency.

• Plant borders – the stalks of grasses and herbaceous plants growing in garden areas are typically much woodier and coarser than the soft plants of lawns and hayfields. Plus, you may wish to grow beds of plants such as stinging nettle or chamomile for teas or tinctures that you intend to harvest by cutting the entire plant. Such plants will damage a scythe edge that has been drawn out too thin, so you will need to peen the edge so that it is robust enough to withstand striking coarser stalks. This can be accomplished by only performing two passes along the edge of the blade (one to bring more material down, one to harden) or by hitting less hard on the first two passes, thus reducing the amount the metal is spread. If you will be mowing very coarse plants on a regular basis, you will probably want a heavier, more robust blade. Because of the extra effort involved in mowing coarse plants, you will want to take smaller 'bites' with each stroke as you mow, which means using a shorter blade.

• Sapling removal and coppicing are jobs for short, robust bush blades. Peen the edge of the blade for maximum robustness and durability, which is to say sharp but not thin and drawn out like a grass blade.

Repairing Nicks

It is pretty much impossible for even the most present, aware mower to avoid occasional damage to the blade caused by striking a stone, a hidden sapling, an exposed tree root, or even the stalk of a tough plant such as stinging nettles. Striking something that isn't grass with a blade sharpened for grass often leads to damage of some sort: bends, cracks, nicks.

Some nicks are repairable through peening, some are not. The deeper the nick (the length/width is not much of an issue), the less likely it can be repaired, with a depth of about 5 mm being the maximum realistically repairable depth. Nicks deeper than 5 mm can render a blade largely unusable, as grass will get stuck in the nicks.

When pounding out a nick through peening, you will only be peening along the length of the blade where the nick is, plus about 2 mm on each side. The idea is to use a 'pulling' hammer stroke to stretch and draw the material from the deepest part of the nick down to the previous position of the edge. First mark either side of the nick using a marker pen **50** .

Since the blade materials should be only slowly drawn down, you will need to peen along the length of the nick several times before it starts to even out with the rest of the edge. Eventually you should be able to pull material down to the point that it hangs down about 1 mm past the position of the edge (test with the edge of a whetstone) 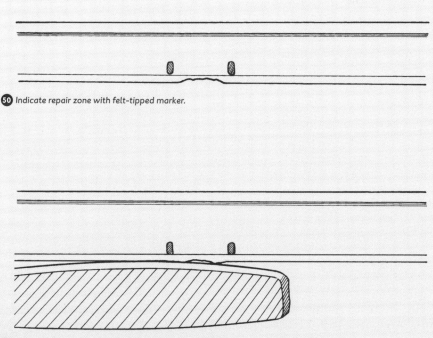. Hone this extra material away with a coarse (ideally artificial) whetstone and observe how the nick has closed to a certain degree. Continue peening and honing off 1 mm 'lips' until the nick has completely closed. Then peen the complete edge of the blade and hone as required.

If you have an older blade that you learned peening on that is now less than perfect because of your earlier lack of peening skills, try making a nick in that blade on purpose and use it to practise smoothing out nicks. The more you work at cold hammering scythe blades, be better your feel for the materials will be and the better your sense for how hard to hit will be.

50 Indicate repair zone with felt-tipped marker.

51 Use a whetstone to test for material spread below edge level. Use a coarse whetstone to remove this extra material.

CHAPTER 7 THE FORGING OF A SCYTHE BLADE

Your enthusiasm for long-term use of the scythe to manage grasslands will depend on your competence in mowing, honing and peening. Knowing what a scythe blade is made of, how it is made and what its strengths and limitations are can help you improve your mowing technique. Mowing as effortlessly as possible is not only important for your body and your ability to mow large fields, it also plays a big part in the effectiveness and longevity of the blade.

Another reason for including this chapter is the fact that top-quality scythes tend to be obtainable only from the European Alps and I would like this to change. The current situation is understandable: the first known scythes are from finds in the Alps, and modern Alpine scythe manufacturers draw on centuries, if not millennia, of unbroken tradition. In areas such as the Alps, the Carpathians and the Pyrenees the use of the scythe has never died out. There are still inhabitants there who require scythes for their livelihoods, are part of a centuries-long unbroken tradition of mowing and know in their bones what they need in a scythe. Elsewhere, this heritage is absent, but I see a potential opportunity for local blacksmiths and others looking to connect with the production of high-quality, sustainably produced food. I hope that by providing some history, background information and technical details, I can inspire blacksmiths in other parts of the world to produce scythes for local needs.

Sickle-like tools from the late Stone Age.

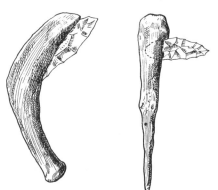

The process of crafting some kind of harvesting blade has evolved over the millennia since the time of the agricultural revolution. It could be said that as long as people have taken food production into their own hands, there have been tools to enable harvesting.

Early Scythes

In central Europe, sickle-like tools with wooden handles and flint blades have been found from the Neolithic era, which commenced with the advent of farming and continued until the invention of metal tools. Egyptian tombs and temples that contain 4000-year-old illustrations are adorned with harvesting scenes featuring workers who hold sickles with one hand to cut stalks of grains bunched together in the other.

The first true sickles appeared in the Bronze Age (bronze being a highly malleable alloy of copper and tin) and they have been found in practically every settlement in Europe dating from this time up until the early Iron Age (700–500 BCE). As bronze is too brittle and heavy to be appropriate for scythes and scythe-like tools, only a few archetypes of what the scythe would later become have been found from the Bronze Age, discovered in ancient pile dwellings in the Italian Alps.

Whereas the sickle is a curved-blade, short-handled tool that is used to cut stalks that have been bundled up with the other hand, a true scythe is a flat (or nearly flat), thin blade that is attached to a long handle held with both hands, has a concave edge that is sharpened for cutting and a convex

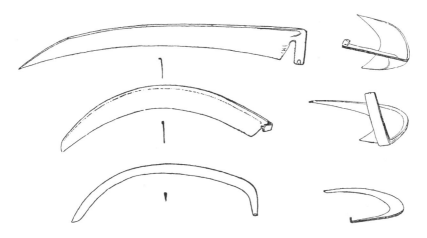

From top to bottom, scythe, short scythe (or Sichte) and gorbushka exemplars.

edge formed for stability and stiffness. A tool that evolved from the sickle and eventually into the scythe is a sort of short scythe called a Sichte in German. The Sichte is attached to a short handle like a sickle but has a scythe-like shape. It differs from both sickle and scythe in its extreme tang angle, which is perpendicular to the plane of the blade.

Another transitional form that was still used in Russia until about a hundred years ago is the gorbuschka – a sabre-like, narrow, yet relatively thick-bladed tool with a wedge-shaped cross section. Its tang is set in the same plane as the blade. Gorbuschki (plural of gorbuschka) were attached to 28–32 in (70–80 cm) handles and mowing was performed while down on one's knees.

The first known true scythes – indeed, the first tools made specifically for harvesting grass – were 16 in (40 cm) long gorbuschka-types from Celtic settlements in modern-day Switzerland, dating from the late La Tène period (second century BC). The combination of the widespread use of

iron at this time – the late Iron Age – and the desire to harvest winter fodder for livestock in cooler, wetter climes that are less appropriate for growing cereals are the basic conditions that led to the invention of the scythe, as cutting grass with a sickle would be tedious to say the least.

Gorbuschka scythes spread to the northeast in the centuries that followed and were slowly replaced by scythes of increasingly refined design. Scythes then essentially disappear from the archaeological record for over a thousand years. We mainly know of their existence through references in official decrees and artwork, so it is difficult to pinpoint exactly when and where specific innovations were made. For example, a manuscript from Salzburg dating to around 800 CE depicts a farmer in the month of July carrying a scythe with a long snath on his shoulder, apparently harvesting hay. Then a further depiction for the month of August shows a farmer harvesting cereals with a sickle. As these are just casual drawings, it is difficult to discern enough detail to confirm or refute the existence of innovations beyond the long snath.

A depiction in a calendar from the mid-10th century shows people harvesting hay with long-snathed gorbuschki. From that time, depictions of scythes and mowers became increasingly common. While many depictions of scythes from 900 to 1200 AD (including those found in reliefs from the main gate of Notre Dame in Paris and the main entrance of Saint Mark's Basilica in Venice) essentially show long-snathed gorbuschki, in the 12th and 13th centuries, depictions of scythes in unmistakably modern forms with wide beards and tangs set at an angle begin to appear, for example in sculptures and stained glass at Chartres Cathedral in France. Thus we can surmise that the scythe we know today came into existence some time around the 12th century.

As for who was making these scythes, official documents with mentions of specialist scythe smiths do not appear until the mid to late 1300s; until then, smiths were considered to be either blacksmiths or blade smiths, the latter presumably being the ones making scythes. By the early 1400s, documentary evidence of larger-scale production and exportation begins to appear in the form of toll collection; a 1409 bill from a trading company in Nuremberg references two barrels full of scythes, one with 600, the other with 535. By the turn of the 16th century, scythe-smithing was an officially recognized profession and scythe smiths began forming guilds.

A typical practice in the early 1500s was for iron mills to produce so-called Sensenknüttel (scythe blade blanks) for local scythe smiths to complete work on and potentially customize blades based on individual preferences. The way this worked was that iron ore was mined in the mountains and crushed into smaller pieces with the use of a stamp mill. These smaller pieces were then further processed at a nearby hammer mill into sword, knife and scythe blanks and other semi-finished pieces with enormous, water-wheel-powered trip hammers. One of the largest workshops at that time, with one master and ten journeymen working purely by hand, was able to produce 70 finished scythes a day from these blanks.

By the mid to late 1500s, because of the iron mills' inability to keep up with demand and scythe smiths' desire not to have their trade infringed upon, smiths started constructing their own relatively small trip hammers in the valleys where they were located in order to produce scythes with materials directly from the stamp mill. This was the first step towards the establishment of scythe works as they exist today, in essence the combination of a small hammer mill and a scythe smith's workshop.

The scythe smiths' trip hammers were originally used just to make blanks, but in 1584, smiths in Micheldorf, Austria, began using them to replace hand hammering in the actual forging (spreading and forming) of scythe blades, which made for a quantum leap in efficiency and quality. Smithies operating by hand quickly disappeared following this innovation and the era of the scythe works began. Indeed, this technological innovation, along with superior Austrian trip-hammer technology and superior metallurgical technique, were the major factors in the Austrian scything industry's rapid ascent to dominance of the world market around the turn of the 17th century – though in the beginning, their efficiency led to market over-saturation that hastened the closing of many small smithies. Austrian scythe works were the first to employ tail helve hammers (tilt hammers), which enabled a much higher stroke rate than the belly helve hammers employed elsewhere until much later. It is the high stroke rate that makes it possible to use them to forge blades in a smoother, more regular shape and more consistent in quality than by hand or with slower belly helve hammers.

The original key consideration for the location of a smithy or scythe works was the presence of sufficient water power to operate a trip hammer and grindstone. Yet the river could not be too large because not only was there no use for the large amounts of power provided by bigger ones, but also the fortifications would be too expensive and the potential for flood damage too great. Sites with rivers having flow rates of about 75–250 gallons (340–1136 litres) per second were the most common for establishing a new workshop.

Another important factor was the presence of trees for making charcoal to fuel the forges. Indeed, after construction of a scythe works, the next building to go up would be a storehouse for six months' worth (or more) of charcoal. Wooden sheds were used for storing, sorting and packing finished scythes because they provided drier conditions than stone ones, thus minimizing the risk of rust to finished blades. Over time,

entire settlements would develop around the scythe works. To minimize the risk of any fire that might occur at the scythe works spreading to nearby buildings, a linden tree (tall and fast-growing) was nearly always planted between the works and other buildings to intercept flying sparks.

The construction of a scythe works began with a weir to alter the flow of the river. Water could then be easily redirected into a sluice for dropping onto a water wheel, thus powering the trip hammers, grindstone and bellows. Weirs were constructed of either driven piles or stone slabs, while water wheels and wooden channels were made of larch and typically lasted about 30 years. Wooden piles for the weir were of fir and could be expected to last 100 years if flooding did not damage them in the meantime.

Water wheels were constructed differently depending on the water flow rate and the angle of slope, but most were at least 8–10 ft (2.4–3 m) in diameter with a paddle width of 2–3 ft (60–90 cm) and operated at 55–100 rpm. They had their own wooden housing to minimize ice accumulation on the wheels in winter. Wheel housings contained 4–5 paddle wheels, as each tool (trip hammers, grindstone, bellows) had its own dedicated paddle wheel.

All in all, a typical scythe works in the 1700s comprised two trip hammers (one for making blanks, the other for forging scythes), a grindstone, four forges (one each for blank production, forging/spreading, hand shaping, and finishing), a tempering trough, a bench for cutting blades to size and a row of anvils for hand shaping.

Steel

The Eisenerz (Iron Ore) Alps in Austria are the source of high-quality, phosphorous-free iron ore which has been the basis for the entire Austrian metalworking industry since the Middle Ages. Originally, iron ore was smelted in the mountains where it was mined in bloomeries – small ovens that turned iron ore into an oxide-free mass of iron and slag called bloom or sponge iron. The temperature of these bloomeries (about 2200°F/1204°C) was not high enough to melt the ore. After about twelve hours of firing, a solid mass of bloom at the floor of the oven was removed with tongs and winches while still glowing white hot. These masses would have the shape of a large round loaf of bread, about 2–3 ft (60–90 cm) in diameter and about 12 in (30.5 cm) thick. Immediately after removal from the bloomery, while still glowing, they would be cut in half with chisels, cut-off hammers and sledge hammers. In the early period of smelting they weighed perhaps 100 lb (45 kg) but by the 1700s they weighed close to half a ton, were the rawest form of iron as a commodity and were sold to hammer mills located on small brooks in the mountain valleys for further processing.

Bloom is a heterogeneous product that consists of outer layers of softer, carbon-poor iron, a core of carbon-rich steel and inclusions of slag and incompletely reduced iron ore. By splintering off each layer separately, steel of varying hardness could be obtained. A bloom chunk was 'baked out' in a hammer mill by heating it to an intense glow and then bringing it under a relatively slow, giant trip hammer to break it up into its different layers, squeeze out slag, improve its structure

and shape material from individual layers into 20–40 lb (9–18 kg) ingots. Material from each layer had its own designated use. For scythes, a middle layer of crude steel (the softest layer that could still be termed steel, containing 0.4–0.6 per cent carbon, and called mock by Austrian scythe smiths) and the hard core steel was used. The larger bloom chunks of the 1700s yielded mostly mock and hard core steel and only low quantities of soft iron and medium-hard steel.

These ingots needed to be further refined to make tools. Hammer mills, then later so-called scrap metal smiths and finally scythe works, hammered these ingots into long bars, which could then be cut down into scythe blanks. Eventually, by the mid-1700s, some scythe works even had their own blast furnaces for refining steel out of pig iron to their own specifications.

Charcoal

Charcoal was just as important as iron for the establishment and survival of a scythe works. Before the Iron Age, territorial princes used forests primarily for hunting. The only other function for a forest, from their perspective, was to provide land for people who would make their living there and then pay taxes to their rulers. As the first ironworkers settled the Alps, the surrounding forests provided the most obvious suitable combustible material.

The annual consumption of charcoal of a scythe works was 378–566 tons, which was the equivalent of up to 4000 cu yd (3058 cu m) of beechwood. Meeting the annual charcoal needs of just one scythe works required up to 1500 acres (607 ha) of relatively slow-growing mountain forest. At one time there were 36 scythe works in Upper Austria alone, meaning that something in the order of 84 sq miles (218 sq km) of forest was dedicated exclusively to the production of charcoal just for these scythe works! Indeed, charcoal production was the primary source of income for many farmers in this area.

Charcoal was the only legal fuel that could provide the high temperatures required in these forges (the use of peat was banned). Furthermore, although charring used up half of the energy of the wood, it also reduced the weight of wood by 75–80 per cent, making it far easier to transport.

Charcoal Production

Woodcutters had close working relationships with charcoal-makers, who were considered to be quaint, contemplative people, perhaps because the pyrolyzing of wood into charcoal needed to be attended to day and night over the course of several weeks. There were plenty of challenges associated with charcoal production, including storms removing the kiln's coating of soil, which needed to be replaced to keep the fire under control.

Charcoal was made by constructing an earth mound kiln. European beech logs (conifer wood was avoided because of its resins) measuring 10 ft (3 m) in length were tightly stacked 4–6 ft (1.2–1.8 m) high and up to 40 yd (36 m) long on a bed of thin limbs laid on firmly tamped clay. This was then walled in by sinking posts and affixing boards, leaving a 9 in (23 cm) gap between the wood to be charred and the wall. Soil and charcoal residues were then used to fill this gap and to top off the mound.

One lower end of the pile was left uncovered, where a fire was lit and kept burning for hours. When the upper layer of logs was sufficiently ablaze, the top of this end was also covered with soil and charcoal residue. The progression of the burn was regulated through the opening and closing of small apertures with a stick, depending on prevailing winds, rain, humidity and so forth. Additional soil or even water was also used to slow piles that burned too vigorously.

A rule of thumb was that the embers of the top of the pile should be about 6 ft (1.8 m) ahead of the embers on the bottom of the pile and the pyrolyzation should not progress more than 6 ft (1.8 m) per day. Large earth mound kilns thus burned for about four weeks. In general, the slower the burn, the better the end product.

Once the fire had progressed 12–18 ft (3.5–5.5 m), the charred portion was reduced to about half its original height and the embers were mostly extinguished, blue smoke would rise from the apertures. This is when the charcoal-maker would begin to take down the boards at this part of the kiln and spread the coals with iron tools to cool. Any remaining embers would be extinguished with water. Completely cooled charcoal was then sieved to separate it from the soil of the mound. Another sieve could then be used to sort the charcoal by size, if desired. The charcoal was then immediately brought into storage to prevent it from getting wet.

A Tour of a Pre-Industrial Scythe Works

In order to understand how scythes were made for almost all of their history, let's now take a tour of a pre-industrial scythe works. The basic production process has not changed significantly in centuries; only the power and precision of the technologies has.

THE BLANK HAMMER Scythe works had a dedicated trip hammer for producing scythe blanks, which were essentially small steel slabs of a specific size, shape and weight. Their helves (the massive 'handles' of the hammers) were December-felled, dried logs of *Fagus sylvatica* (European or common beech) 9 ft (2.7 m) in length and 10 in

(25 cm) in diameter. The helves were fitted with two cast iron reinforcement rings called hursts (one 80 lb [36 kg] hurst at the pivot point, one 25–30 lb [11.5–13.5 kg] hurst where the helve meets the cam) and a cast iron head weighing 120–150 lb (54.5–68 kg). The hammer struck an 80 lb (36 kg) anvil that was set in a 350–400 lb (159–181 kg) anvil block, which was in turn set in a nearly vertical oak log with its own iron reinforcement ring and set 6 ft (1.8 m) deep into the ground.

The hammer was powered by an eight- to ten-toothed cam attached to a 20 in (50 cm) diameter cam shaft. Underneath the cam end

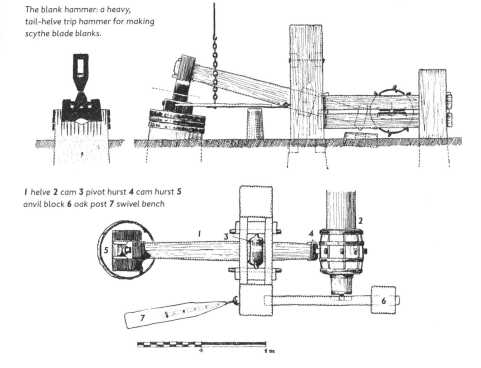

The blank hammer: a heavy, tail-helve trip hammer for making scythe blade blanks.

1 helve 2 cam 3 pivot hurst 4 cam hurst 5 anvil block 6 oak post 7 swivel bench

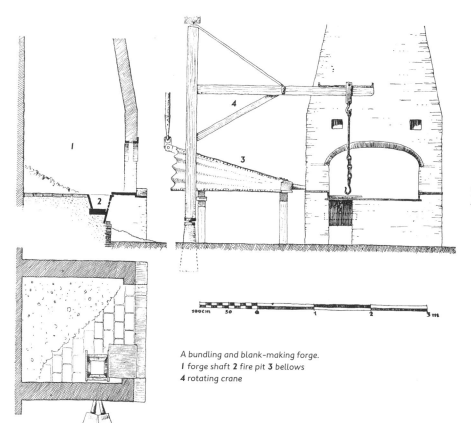

A bundling and blank-making forge.
1 forge shaft **2** fire pit **3** bellows
4 rotating crane

of the helve, a barrier plate prevented the hammer head from being raised too high and provided for a bouncing effect that increased the speed of the hammer. Hammers for blank production were set up to make 280 strokes per minute, which stressed helves to the extent that they needed to be changed every few weeks (sometimes even after a few days) because of cracking. The smith sat to the side of the hammer head on a swivelling bench hooked to the frame of the hammer and attached to a ceiling joist with a chain.

THE BLANK FORGE The forge for blank-making was located near the blank hammer. It was essentially a square-shaped vertical brick shaft about 6 ft (1.8 m) deep with a chimney on top. The heating surface was about 2 ft (60 cm) above the floor, constructed of brick, and its opening faced the hammer (it provided light for the hammersmith in insufficient daylight). The forge had a waterwheel-powered bellows associated with it. A boom crane was used to move work pieces in and out of the forge.

THE DRAWING HAMMER For the forging of a scythe, where the steel of a blank is drawn out by hammering to form a thin flat blade, another dedicated trip hammer with different specifications was used. It was constructed nearly the same as the hammer for blank production, but had a heavier head (160 lb/72.5 kg) with a substantially narrower striking face that was set up to strike 180 times per minute. Another important difference between the blank hammer and the drawing hammer was the control the smith had over the speed of the drawing hammer. This was done with an iron lever that regulated the flow of water to the paddle wheel. In contrast to the blank hammer, the smith would sit directly in front of the drawing hammer on a low stool.

THE DRAWING FORGE The drawing forge was built much like the blank forge, but smaller. The point of this forge was to heat about half the length of inserted scythes as evenly as possible.

Grindstones for scythes were of extremely hard Rieselberger sandstone.

THE HARDENING SHOP This also had its own dedicated forge with water-wheel-powered bellows for a perpetual intense fire. The other key element was a copper hardening trough, itself contained in a secondary wooden trough. It had to be continually flushed with fresh water so that melted beef tallow in the trough, which helped prevent blades from cracking in the hardening trough, did not become too hot as burning scythes were repeatedly plunged in the water. The trough was fitted with an iron plate for placing scythes removed from the trough and a box of sawdust for removing tallow adhering to the blades.

THE GRINDSTONE The Rieselberger sandstone grindstone was about 4 ft (1.2 m) in diameter and 12 in (30½ cm) thick. It spun at 100 revolutions per minute and was irrigated by small wooden troughs and rills while in operation.

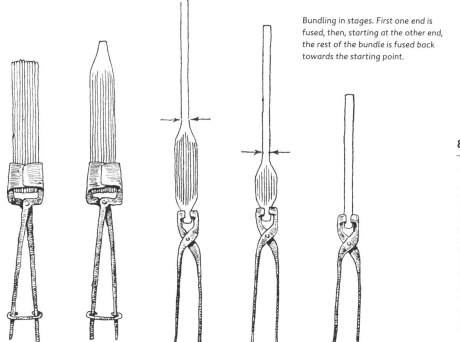

Bundling in stages. First one end is fused, then, starting at the other end, the rest of the bundle is fused back towards the starting point.

THE SCYTHING HANDBOOK

BUNDLING Scythe works took on steels of varying hardnesses and processed them to make blanks for scythe production. To do this, they bundled different kinds of steel together, heated these bundles and then welded them together to make scythe blanks.

To bundle different kinds of steel, long strips of each kind were made by separately heating ingots of each kind of steel in the scythe works' largest forge and hammering the heated steel into long, flat slabs of about ⅓–2 in (0.8–5 cm) thickness under the blank production hammer. This was done by first making a 'tail' by hammering one end, then gripping this tail with the tongs and hammering the rest. Immediately after completion, this slab of raw steel would be notched with a wedge hammer at 2 ft (60 cm) intervals and tossed in a vat of water for hardening. This work was typically done in the evening to set up smiths for the following day. Since bundling was the forging work that required the least amount of skill, it was the task used to introduce apprentices to forging on the trip hammer.

The actual bundling of thin slabs of steel was the process of stacking 9–15 slabs of soft steel for chine bundles (4–6 strips of hard steel for cutting edge bundles) and clamping them together with special bundling tongs, the jaws of which tightly girded all the rails and locked shut with a clamping ring. This bundle was then placed in the blank forge and removed when glowing sufficiently by the stoker (the person operating the forge), who then hand-hammered the ends of the bundles to lightly weld them together to prevent slippage of the slabs. The stoker then 'tipped' the bundle by completely welding one end under the blank hammer.

The bundle, weighing upwards of 40 lb (18 kg), was then returned to the forge with the non-tipped end in the fire, where it was coated in clay slip or powdered clay to promote fusion of the bundled slabs. When the bundle was hot enough for welding, the hammersmith took the bundle with another set of tongs at the tipped end and used the blank hammer to weld about a third of the length of the bundle into a 1 x 1 in (2.5 x 2.5 cm) rod of steel (half as thick for cutting edge steel) about 3 ft (90 cm) in length. This rod was then chiselled off and tossed in a vat of water while still hot. The rest of the bundle was returned to the fire and two more rods could be made from it. Since these bundles were so heavy, hammersmiths sat on movable wooden benches to the side of the hammer head where they could support the tongs on their knees, which were protected by a leather apron.

The point of this exercise was to mix together heterogeneous raw materials to make them usable to forge scythe blades. In this way, harder, more carbon-rich steel was welded with softer, carbon-poorer steel, which improved the overall structure of the steel, squeezed out slag residues and evened out the carbon contents of adjacent components of the bundle. The aim was to end up with the desired carbon content, which was accomplished not only by selecting the right mixture of raw steel components for the

bundles, but also by skilled use of the bellows in the forge. The more horizontal or downwards the bellows blew, the more the steel was decarbonized and thus made softer and vice versa. Finished bundles were then broken into pieces about 4 in (10 cm) long, depending on the intended length of the finished blade, by first notching them, then inserting them into a perfectly fitted hole in an iron block up to the notch and finally striking off with a sledgehammer, thus producing the straightest possible break.

Since there were two kinds of bundles being made – softer steel for the chine, harder steel for the cutting edge – one piece of each needed to be paired so that their combined weight was the desired weight for the blade being made. Every manufacturer had their own ratios of hard and soft steel. At the extreme, perhaps only one-eighth of the blade's steel would be hard, meaning that only the outer cutting edge was hard steel and the rest of the blade was soft. Such a blade lasted only for a year or two under regular use. Other blades, with twice as much hard steel (a quarter of the blade by weight), lasted three to five times longer.

In pre-industrial times, bundling was a crucial part of the scythe forging process because of the heterogeneous nature of the raw materials they worked with. A lot of thought and attention went into the unique qualities of each batch of new raw materials brought into the forge. Modern blades use hard edge steel for the entire blade. This steel can be ordered to exact specifications (the specific contents of carbon and other minerals are often closely-guarded secrets) from steel companies.

COMBINING BUNDLES TO MAKE BLANKS AND FORGING THE TANG

A stoker heats blade blanks in the blank forge using tongs.

A scythe blade blank was made by fusing a soft piece for the body with a hard piece for the cutting edge. One piece of each was taken in a pair of tongs that were locked shut with a clamping ring and placed in the blank forge. The stoker would then weld each end together by striking with a hand hammer when the pair was hot enough. Then the stoker used the blank hammer to weld the entire pair together and spread half to make a flat bar ¼-½ in (6–13 mm) thick, depending on the type of blade to be made. This in-between product went by a name in German that will be familiar to agricultural toy enthusiasts: Ertl.

The Ertl was then put right back into the forge to heat the side that was clamped in the tongs and thus not completely welded. The hammersmith would take the piece and forge the tang with the blank hammer, paying attention to which side the hard steel was on so as to have the tang pointing in the right direction. Some scythe works would make their Ertl with a shorter piece of hard steel so the tang could be made only of soft steel. Finally, the knob at the end of the tang was typically shaped with hand hammers.

DRAWING OUT THE BLADE These slabs of welded steel with forged tangs were then heated in the drawing forge almost all the way to the tang, then brought under the drawing hammer to be made into scythe blades. The tang (which had not been heated but was hot to the touch) was held with a cloth or glove in the left hand and the piece was stabilized by holding it with tongs in the right hand. By passing the still glowing piece evenly under the hammer, the steel was drawn out to form the blade, while the

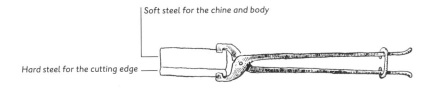

Soft steel for the chine and body

Hard steel for the cutting edge

An overview of the stages of
combining soft and hard steel,
forging the tang and forging the
knob to make scythe blade blanks.

Forging the tang

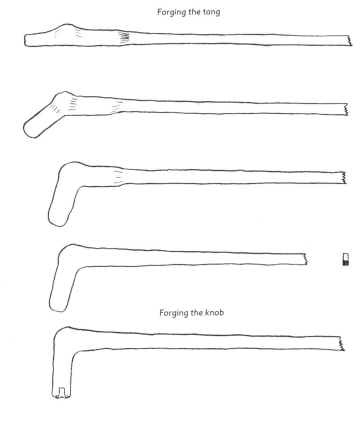

Forging the knob

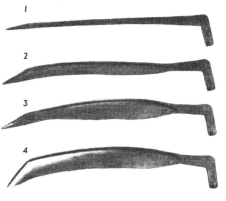

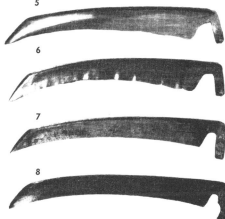

Drawing out the blade
1 Blank with tang and knob 2 First drawing out
3 Second drawing out 4 Forged point
5 Forged beard 6 Formed chine 7 Cut, smoothed,
tempered, shaped and honed ('grey') blade
8 Finished, painted ('blue') blade.

portion that was to form the chine was left untouched at this point. This first phase of drawing out resulted in a piece that was about 1½ in (38 mm) wide and about ⅛ in (4 mm) thick all the way down to the point, excluding the first quarter of the length of the piece which was neither heated nor hammered at this stage.

When all the pieces had been through the first phase of drawing out, the drawing hammer's face was honed for the next phase. The pieces were replaced in the forge to heat primarily their middle portions and then brought under the hammer again – this time flipped over with the chine-to-be on the left side and then quickly flipped over again between hammer strikes to ensure even thickness of the blade.

The blade was heated a third time at the point and the point was then forged under the hammer as in the second phase: first

upside down, then right side up. Finally, the blade was heated a fourth time at the tang so that the beard could be forged. The heels of the tang and the beard were often reinforced during this phase, either with a 'stag's tongue' – a finger-long, tapered rib parallel to the chine originating at the tang – or by simply forging the heel so that the material was less drawn out and thus stronger.

Very short blades could be forged with just three heatings whereas especially long scythes required an extra heating because the blade would cool too quickly to draw out along the entire length. For especially wide blades, like those traditionally used in France and Spain where the beard could be up to 8 in (20 cm) wide, the beard was forged in two heatings to prevent cracking. Material was drawn out after the first heating with a bulge at the end. After the second heating, this bulge of steel was drawn out to complete the beard.

Forging the heel

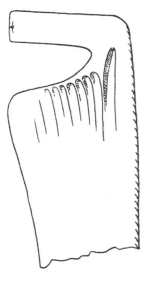

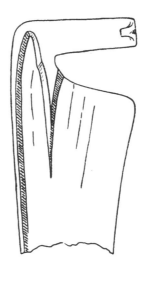

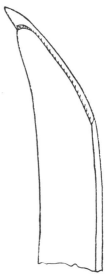

Crown-style beard reinforcement.

'Stag's tongue'-style beard reinforcement.

Reinforced point of special blades made for rocky soils.

At this point the material of the blade was fully drawn out and some of the most important features of the blade (curvature and thickness of the chine, thickness and consistency of the blade) were established.

FORMING THE CHINE A turned-up chine, at a right angle to the plane of the blade, is what gives the blade its rigidity, in the same way that a piece of angle iron gets its strength from its shape. In pre-industrial times, a dedicated forge was used to this end. The chine was formed in two stages. In the first stage, the tang half of the blade was brought to a red heat in the forge, then turned up with hand hammers and a specially shaped anvil. In the second stage, the point half of the blade was heated and then the chine was turned up.

At this point, hand hammers and anvils were used to shape the blades to conform to the design of the particular scythe being made.

FINISHING A number of small tasks were then performed to finish each blade. The edge was cut with a simple alligator (or lever) shear to ensure the exact width of the blade with no notches. The tang would be heated and imprinted with a maker's mark using an engraved mark hammer that was placed on the tang and hit with a sledge. Then the tang angle was set. Blades at this stage were called 'grey' blades in that they were in their final shape, but not yet tempered.

The blade would be heated until it reached an even, yellow heat. Then it was removed and immediately stroked along the entire length with a bar that smoothed out any folds or inconsistencies. Then the blade was dunked chine-first into the molten beef tallow of the tempering trough. Once cooled, the blade was removed and cleaned of tallow with a spatula-shaped, wetted piece of tree bark, then put in a box of sawdust to remove what was left of the tallow. Finally, the blade was heated again a little, then tossed in a trough of cold water. Firescale (a layer of oxides that forms on the surface of metals when heated) would literally jump off the blade at this point. When firescale completely jumped off, leaving a blade with an even, light grey sheen, this was considered an indication of high-quality steel.

It was only after tempering that the blade was given its curvature in the vertical dimension (from the perspective of the blade being on the ground). It was rasped for smoothness, then passed on to a row of hammerers, each one altering the shape slightly before handing on to the next. The final hammerer was the master and had final say as to whether a blade was in the correct 'pose' or not.

The blade was then honed with an irrigated whetstone (with final peening to be done by the farmer) before one final adjustment with hammer and anvil, as honing could cause some distortion in the blade. And with that, the blade was finished.

Obviously, it's not practical for anyone to set up a water-powered scythe works in this modern world. Furthermore, iron ore is no longer refined in bloomeries and modern scythe works make blades that consist entirely of hard edge steel. My hope is that by describing everything that was traditionally involved in manufacturing a scythe, I might inspire modern-day blacksmiths to work out how they can use their modern equipment to execute the same tasks that were performed for centuries in the service of agrarian societies.

CHAPTER 8 MAKING HAY AND USING DRYING RACKS

When I first started making hay by hand, the only thing I had to go by was my experiences making hay with machines in Austria. When the grass was long enough and three consecutive rain-free days were forecast, hay fields were mown on the first day and the mown grass was raked evenly across the field to dry under the sun. At the end of the day, the hay was raked into windrows for the night, which reduced the amount of cut grass exposed to morning dew.

The next day, the hay was spread out evenly across the field again to maximize exposure to the drying sun, a process known as tedding. At the end of the second day, the drying grass was again raked into windrows by tractor.

On the third day, the windrows were tedded one last time and the grass was allowed to dry for one more half day. After lunch, the cut grass, now completely dried into hay, was raked one last time into windrows and then baled with a small square baler and stacked on the wagon being pulled from behind.

Hay-making by hand

I had a lot of fun making hay. Once I decided to start doing it by hand, this model of making hay by machine was the only point of reference I had except one. One day, while driving from southern Austria to Linz, I saw a small farm where a man and woman were taking hay from various stacks in a field with a hay fork and, in graceful motions that they had certainly repeated millions of times in their lifetimes, they tossed and fluffed the hay onto the ground, where it landed perfectly spread out. They were basically doing what I had learned to do by machine, but by hand. On talking to them I discovered that at night they would stack the hay to minimize the surface area of the grass that was exposed to dew, then in the morning they would spread it out again, thus mixing it and maximizing sun exposure.

Back in the USA, living on a homestead in Iowa, I decided to make hay by hand myself, using a scythe, hay fork and hand rake. I would wake up as early in the morning as I could to maximize the amount of time I had to mow dew-coated grass before the sun came up and dried it out. Once the morning's mowing was done, I grabbed the hay fork and fluffed and tedded the cut grass that was still lying in windrows, spreading it around the field as evenly as I could. I tried to emulate those farmers I saw in Austria, who seemed to distribute the hay effortlessly, but I definitely had to put plenty of effort into it. At night I would rake the hay into windrows, in the morning I would ted it again. On the third day, I raked the hay into windrows and gathered it up on the fork by just walking down the windrows with the fork on the ground ahead of me. I loaded it on a garden cart and carried it to a big pile, load by load.

This works, but it is pretty labour-intensive. Even if you were able to mow an acre or two per day, tedding and raking, with mowing, would make for a really big, exhausting job, and at the end of it you would not have a great deal of hay. And at that point you would probably not want to look at a scythe, fork and rake again for a long time.

Continuous Hay-making with Drying Racks

Fortunately there are other drying methods that do not require all that tedding and raking and they make for higher quality hay, too. Stacking cut grass on a rack to cure into hay, done well, protects from rain (which would otherwise wash out nutrients from the cut grass, necessitate longer drying times and perhaps cause mould and/or rotting) and eliminates the need to ted and rake, which frees you up to spend more of your day mowing and allows you to do it any day the weather is suitable. In this way it is possible to make small amounts of hay more or less every day of the season which, little by little, adds up to your animals' winter feed store. Mowing, racking and loading cured hay into the hay mow can just be part of your morning chores and you no longer need to stress about weather and a huge workload for three days, two or three times a year.

Loading a cart with hay

The instinctive way to load a small garden cart with hay is just to pitch it right in the middle every time. But as the pile rises it quickly develops a rounded top, even if you continually press it down. Eventually, the lack of flat surface on top of the pile makes it impossible to stack more without it all falling down the sides. Instead, try loading the cart by shoving forkfuls of hay only in the corners, one after another, in sequence. As the piles rise, the bulk of the hay is focused on each corner, forming a stable tower. Stacking this way, you can keep going up and up; the top will always be broad and flat, so no hay falls down the sides. Adding flanges to the top of the cart increases the amount you can stack by effectively widening the cart.

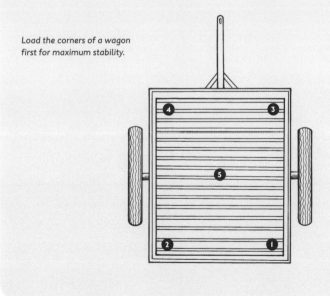

Load the corners of a wagon first for maximum stability.

Nutrient Loss when Drying Hay on the Ground

Even when hay is made in perfect weather, there are significant losses of nutrients in the grass that occur between the time the grass is mown and when the hay is finally consumed by livestock. Indeed, studies have indicated losses of 40 per cent of starches and a third of the protein that were present in the grass before cutting. Significant drops in the quality of the hay compared to living pasture grass is a primary reason for the need to supplement livestock diets with concentrated feed in the winter. If we were able to preserve all the nutrients that are present all season long in pasture grass in hay, it would be unnecessary to import winter feed.

There are seven main reasons for nutrient losses in hay made by curing on the ground:

1 RESPIRATION When grass is cut, the uptake of nutrients to the parts above the cut is stopped, yet cell respiration continues until the cells die, using energy from nutrients present in the cut blades of grass. The more unevenly the grass dries and the longer moisture remains in the grass, the greater the respiration losses. The faster the grass dries, the faster cells die, the lower the respiration losses. Respiration losses are minimal (around 10 per cent) when hay cures under ideal conditions, but begin to rise (15 per cent or more) as humidity increases and winds decrease.

2 PHYSICAL DETERIORATION AND LEAF SHATTER OF CURED HAY Delicate, leafy plants such as clover and alfalfa that have been dried to a very low moisture content are more likely to shatter, turn to dust and fall to the ground or blow away when being taken

off the field. The more the hay has been raked, tedded and windrowed during curing, the higher the nutrient losses due to leaf shatter. This is especially true of second or third cuttings of grass hay and clover hay of any cutting, the shattered leaves of which can be seen covering the ground after loading the hay into wagons. No matter how careful you are, nutrient losses of this sort are essentially unavoidable when drying hay on the ground.

3 WASHOUT BY RAIN Readily soluble nutrients in hay are dissolved and washed away by rainfall. The further along the hay is in the curing process – that is, the drier it is – the greater the potential nutrient losses from washout. So, rain washes out fewer nutrients from freshly cut grass than from grass that has dried almost enough to be brought into storage. A short storm washes out fewer nutrients than a light rain that lasts all day. When drying hay on the ground, raking into windrows or small piles reduces the overall surface area of cut grass exposed to rain. Since no one is perfect, this step will inevitably be neglected sooner or later and in any case windrows or small piles can only provide so much protection against longer periods of rain, so you will have to reckon with washout losses at some point or other if drying on the ground is the strategy you choose to make hay.

4 SOIL MOISTURE AND RESULTANT MOULD GROWTH Mould can have a deteriorating effect on aromatic substances in the hay, which can in turn reduce the hay's ability to stimulate the appetite of livestock. Windrowing or piling curing grass during rain helps protect against washout, but this can also encourage moulding. Plus, spreading grass out to dry on mown meadow that has just been rained upon traps moisture, which also encourages mould.

5 FERMENTATION AND OVERHEATING IN STORAGE Curing and bringing in your hay does not mean that the risk of nutrient loss is gone. As grass cures into hay, moisture trapped in the cells under more or less anaerobic conditions leads to fermentation. This warms the hay, which can affect the digestibility of its protein, and even heat it to the point where it chars or bursts into flames. Ground-cured hay, brought in after 2–3 days, is more likely to undergo an intense, heat-producing fermentation in storage than is rack-cured hay that is brought in after 8–10 days having already undergone a cooler, less intense fermentation process.

6 MOULDING IN STORAGE If hay is brought in before it is dry enough or if it gets rained on while being brought in, it is very likely to get mouldy in storage. Mouldy hay not only lacks nutrition compared to non-mouldy hay, it is also hazardous to your animals' health.

7 ALLOWING GRASS TO GROW TOO LONG BEFORE MOWING This can easily occur if rain comes when it is time to make hay. The timing of mowing is critical for the protein content of the resultant hay. The further the plants progress towards blossoming and seed formation, the more raw fibre and the less digestible protein they contain. Indeed, if mowing is postponed by a week or more, digestible nutrients, especially protein, can decrease by 30–40 per cent. Once the rain stops, you will probably have to speed the hay-making process along as much as possible, which then risks moulding of the hay in storage.

As you can see, making hay by drying it on the ground may seem easy, but it comes with a host of disadvantages, even when hay-making weather is ideal. Losses can be immense when rainy weather comes into play, endangering not only spread and windrowed grass, but even the standing grass that is yet to be mowed. If your goal is to produce winter fodder for your livestock that approximates the nutrition of summer forage, drying hay on the ground will not produce the quality of feed that you require.

Advantages of Drying on Hay Racks

To avoid the drawbacks of drying hay on the ground, we need a convenient method for curing hay that does not require perfect weather and is neither prohibitively expensive nor requires more work. It should be cheap and accessible to anyone and ensure the production of high-quality winter fodder by drying hay quickly and evenly, reducing the need to move the hay to minimize leaf shatter; it should shed rain and keep the intensity of fermentation to a minimum.

Curing hay with hay racks meets all these criteria. In fact, it has long rendered high-quality hay-making possible in remote mountain valleys in the Alps, where frequent rainfall makes ground-dried hay unfeasible. The idea behind all hay racks is to keep grass up off the ground as it dries, encourage it to shed rain and increase the grass's exposure to drying winds. There are three main designs

for hay racks: hay-drying poles, quadripods and wire/pole racks.

Hay-making with racks keeps nutrient losses to a minimum, reduces the amount of work required to cure hay and frees you from dependence on the weather. The resultant high-quality hay increases your livestock's appetite, which means that not only is the hay more nutritious, your animals will eat more of it, which increases production without the need to import feed. According to Professor Ivins in André Voisin's book *Grass Productivity*, 'Palatability is the sum of the factors which operate to determine whether, and to what degree, the food is attractive to the animal; it can thus be held to constitute the connecting link between grass and the grazing animal and is regarded by various authors to be of greater importance than nutritive value. Necessarily relative, it is influenced by such variables as the animal itself, stage of growth and development of the herbage, alternative foods and the management and manuring of the herbage.'

Loose haystack on ground (left), Tyrolean pole (middle), basic pole (right).

Comparison of Curing Methods

As imports of concentrated animal feed increased in Switzerland in the early part of the 20th century, a group of professors from Swiss agricultural schools conducted a study comparing hay cured on the ground (the standard method at the time) with hay cured on racks (a then relatively new, not yet widespread method), in order to tease out the concrete benefits of the latter. The results of their investigations, conducted in the years 1928–30, were as follows:

1 The moisture content of the hay as it enters storage is a critical factor in its performance in storage. A moisture content above 25 per cent all but guarantees mould growth in the hay. For all trials, the average moisture content of racked hay was 17.9–24.3 per cent compared with 24.1–26.5 per cent for ground-cured hay. In other words, hay cured on racks presented a reduced risk of mould growth and overheating compared with hay cured on the ground. The curing of hay on racks consistently yielded a more aromatic, nutrient-rich, health-enhancing feed than hay that was cured on the ground.

2 A significant reduction in nutrient losses for rack-cured hay was observed throughout the study. In the chart below, notice the reduction in nutrient losses in the racked hay even in good weather. And if you find the loss numbers even for rack-cured hay disturbing, think about the amount of hay that you will be making every year; losing 39 per cent of starch instead of 45 per cent amounts to quite a bit of starch when considering the big picture. Drying on the ground during the trials was done by the book – that is, they did not mow if it was about to rain and hay was always windrowed when rain threatened. Differences between ground-cured and rack-cured hay are probably even greater in reality because ground curing is almost never implemented so perfectly as it was in this study.

	Good Hay-making Weather		Rain	
	% Protein Lost	% Starch Lost	% Protein Lost	% Starch Lost
Curing on ground	32.86	41.58	39.54	45.36
Curing on rack	27.62	37.18	31.79	39.18

Basic hay drying poles: cylindrical in form, loosely loaded, close to ground without touching, lightly capped with hay.

In addition to the curing trials, feeding trials with each kind of hay were undertaken. In digestibility tests conducted by the ETH Zürich (Swiss Federal Institute of Technology Zurich), the nutrients in rack-cured hay were more digestible than those in ground-cured hay. In tests with dairy cows, appetite stimulation and milk yields were significantly higher for rack-cured hay. The use of racks not only protects against nutrient losses, it also ensures high quality and high digestibility in the finished product. Increased appetites mean increased quantities of hay eaten and a proportional reduction in imported feed.

The amount of labour required to windrow and spread hay on the ground even once is more than the labour required to load racks once. Therefore, if you are absolutely positive you are not going to need to windrow ground-cured hay, you would save labour by curing on the ground. As soon as you have to windrow the hay once, though, you are using more labour than you would have if you had racked the hay, to say nothing of the times where two or three windrowings are required to cure the hay because of unexpected precipitation. When you also

consider the time and effort to get to the field and back, the cost of the time and effort put into windrowing, the use of helpers and so forth, the costs of the choice to cure on the ground can be high.

The main burden of rack-curing hay is the acquisition or construction of equipment. The rack designs described later in this chapter are all intended to be easy to build from materials on your own land or from recycled sources. Still, depending on how much hay you make, you may have to build a lot of racks.

In summary, curing hay on racks makes for better hay than curing on the ground. on some occasions, you may save a bit of work by ground curing and, provided it doesn't rain, you will not have made huge sacrifices in hay quality. Once you are set up to use racks, you will, on average, make higher quality, more nutritious hay, import less winter feed and put less work into making your hay.

Hay Rack Designs

The earliest hay rack design was the hay-drying pole (German: Heinze, from Heuzähne 'hay teeth'), originally made of small fir trees with their branches cut back to about 8 in (20 cm) in length to support the grass they were to be loaded with. Eventually these were constructed from milled lumber with rungs built in to support grass. A tripod can be made of three hay-drying poles. A relatively more recent innovation are quadripods (German: Hütten 'huts'), made of two ladder-like frames bound together at the top to form a construction resembling an A-frame. They can be designed to allow for folding together for easier transport and storage. In Sweden and other northern European countries, long, continuous wire racks were developed. After loading with hay, they appear in the fields as long walls of hung grass. Originally made of wooden posts, they can also be made with metal T-posts, which can be easier to deal with and last much longer.

Despite the variation in design and construction, all hay racks are intended to get cut grass off the ground, increase the grass's exposure to wind and reduce its exposure to rain by minimizing the overall surface area directly exposed to rain and shedding what rain falls on them. For larger racks, it is ideal to let the grass dry somewhat before loading. Smaller racks are better able to dry freshly cut, maximally wet grass. It can be tempting to load as much grass as possible onto a rack to minimize the number of racks used, but racks need to be packed lightly enough to cure grass deep inside, especially if it rains all day some time before the hay cures and moisture finds its way to even the deepest-buried grass. What follows is a summary of the classic styles of racks for drying cut grass into hay, adapted from Landis's *Die verbesserte Dürrfutterernte*.

A stand of well-built Tyrolean poles. Note the space between hay and ground, which prevents wicking of ground moisture.

BASIC HAY-DRYING POLE

CONSTRUCTION The basic hay-drying pole consists of a 5 ft (1.5 m) long, 1½–2 in (4–5 cm) thick pole (roundwood with bark removed or milled lumber), pointed at the bottom for driving into the ground. At 2 ft (60 cm), 3ft (90 cm) and 4 ft (125 cm) from the point, 1½ x ½ in (4 x 1 cm) rungs about 20 in (50 cm) in length are tightly attached, each oriented 90 degrees from each other (top and bottom rung face the same direction). Dimensional lumber holds hay better than does roundwood for the rungs.

NUMBER REQUIRED PER ACRE (HECTARE) 360–600 (900–1500)

INSTALLATION IN THE FIELD Pound into the ground with a wooden or rubber sledge hammer or mallet. Orient the top and bottom rungs towards prevailing winds.

LOADING Easier with two people, but one person can load the poles alone. Bundle together the hay nearest the pole and start with the lowest rung, alternating loading against and with the wind so that the bundles lock each other in place. Proceed upward to the top rung. Inspect the poles daily in windy weather to ensure the hay has not blown off. Make tripods with poles for shorter grass (from second or third cutting). Rake underneath to ensure no contact between the ground and the racked grass.

UNLOADING Wait until the hay is dry enough for storage to unload. Pick up the entire pole by gently moving it to and fro as you pull it up. Shake the hay onto the ground or directly into the wagon.

PROS Can be used for very wet (even dewy or rain-soaked) grass. Light, airy loading makes it possible to make decent hay in any weather. Adaptable to any terrain and easy to use.

CONS Large numbers of poles required, potentially difficult to transport and store, rungs break easily, labour-intensive.

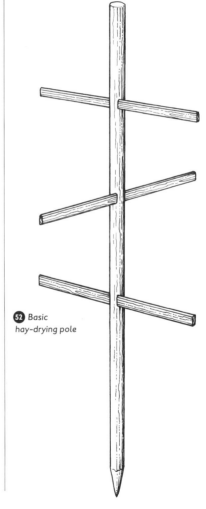

52 Basic hay-drying pole

TYROLEAN HAY-DRYING POLE

CONSTRUCTION A 9 ft (2.7 m) long fir pole, 2½ in (6.5 cm) in diameter, pointed top and bottom with removable rungs. Bottom point 4–6 in (10–15 cm) long, top point 8–12 in (20–30 cm) long. To install the rungs, bore pairs of elongated ovals through the pole, about ½ in (1 cm) wide, 1¼–1½ in (3–4 cm) tall. Make each pair at right angles with one another. For the first pair, one hole at 1 ft 4 in (40 cm), the other at 1 ft 6 in (46 cm) from the bottom tip, the next pair 2 ft (60 cm) above the highest hole from the previous level, then one final rung 2 ft (60 cm) above the previous pair. Make rungs 2 ft (60 cm) long, tapered at the bottom of both ends. All holes and rungs should be of the same size and fit tightly.

NUMBER REQUIRED PER ACRE (HECTARE) 80–160 (200–400)

INSTALLATION IN THE FIELD With a post-hole digging bar with a 5 ft (1.5 m) handle and a point on one end, make a hole about 12 in (30 cm) deep, press the hay-drying pole into the ground and tamp the ground around the pole with the feet and head of the post-hole digging bar. Insert the two lowest rungs. If installing multiple poles before loading, leave the other three rungs at base of each pole. Make rows with 3–4 yd (2.7–3.6 m) spacing between and within rows (more or less, depending on amount of grass).

LOADING With a hay fork, place small forkloads of hay on each rung half, one at a time, and stack upwards until reaching the next holes. Insert the next two rungs and continue stacking, one small forkload after

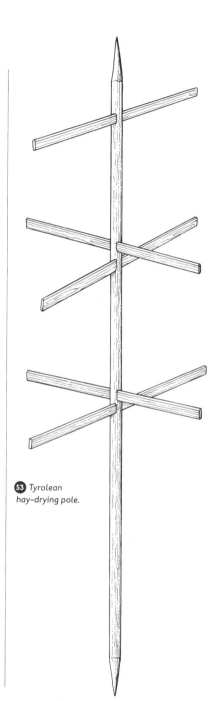

53 Tyrolean hay-drying pole.

another. Stack the grass as fluffily and airily as possible and never plop the hay down with the weight of the fork. The final rung is simply a kind of cap that holds the whole thing together and the top point of the pole should be hidden in the airily piled grass. The entire loaded pole should be as loose as possible, with no grass pressed together; the finished pole should be cylindrical in shape (not conical, which increases the surface area exposed to rain), slender and free of the ground. Rake underneath to ensure there is no contact between ground and racked grass.

UNLOADING Grass should remain on the pole until it is dry enough for storage, at least four days, up to 10–14 depending on the weather. The poles can be unloaded from above with a hay fork wielded by someone standing on a wagon or the rungs can be removed, freeing the hay to fall to the ground in a pile, whence it can be loaded into a wagon or cart with a hayfork.

PROS Easy to store, easy to transport and install in the field, completely made of wood (no wire or nails), can be used to dry sheaves of small grains.

CONS Pre-drying is required to avoid slumping of grass and moulding of grass at the bottom. Nearly impossible to use where thin, stony soils prevail.

QUADRIPOD

CONSTRUCTION Quadripods are four-legged, collapsible racks composed of two halves that lean together and may be connected at the top with a bolt or threaded rod. Each half is fitted with four horizontal crossbars for holding hay. When collapsed, the rack is about 6½ ft (2 m) tall, but the poles or boards used to make the frame are about 7 ft (2.1 m) long and 6 ft (1.8 m) apart at the base; the lower crossbar is 6½ ft (2 m) long, the middle crossbar about 6 ft (1.8 m), the top crossbar 5 ft 3 in (1.6 m). The crossbars are spaced about 12 in (30 cm) apart, with the bottom crossbar at least 2 ft (60 cm) off the ground. Traditionally, quadripods were made of fir branches 2–3 in (5–7.5 cm) in diameter, thicker branches for the frame, thinner for the crossbars. Fasten as convenient: lashing, dowels, screws and so on. Wire can be used for the crossbars to reduce weight. Too much spacing between the crossbars necessitates overloading each crossbar with grass so it does not fall off. This, however, often leads to mould growth. It is better to have more crossbars at closer spacing between the bars (and thus more loosely packed grass) than fewer crossbars with denser packing of grass.

NUMBER REQUIRED PER ACRE (HECTARE) 30–60 (75–150), more required for rain-soaked grass, fewer for grass dried for one day.

INSTALLATION IN THE FIELD Establish 6½ ft (2 m) paths every 10–15 yd (9–14 m) for rows of quadripods. Transport multiple quadripods with a wagon, single by hand or with a wheelbarrow. Set up so the prevailing winds blow through the triangular opening.

LOADING One person on each side makes for faster loading. Start with one hayfork load of grass for each outer end of the lower crossbar, then fill the middle with 1–2 fork loads. Do not turn the fork as you load; hold it in the same position you used to get hay on the fork. For the top crossbar, start in the middle and work your way out to the ends, overlapping like roof shingles. Fill holes as needed and remove blades of grass that hang down to the ground by 'sweeping' with the hay fork. Use this extra grass to form a cap at the top of the rack, but do not make a cap when grass is soaked with rain. The wetter the grass, the less should be loaded onto the rack. Common mistakes are: overloading the quadripod; making the cap too large and too dense; overhanging the gable ends too much, which obstructs airflow; leaving gaps in grass hung on crossbars instead of forming a solid wall.

UNLOADING Grass should remain on the quadripod until it is dry enough for storage, at least four days, eight or more in volatile weather. It may be tempting to unload the quadripod and ted the grass on the ground again after it rains, but this extra step is

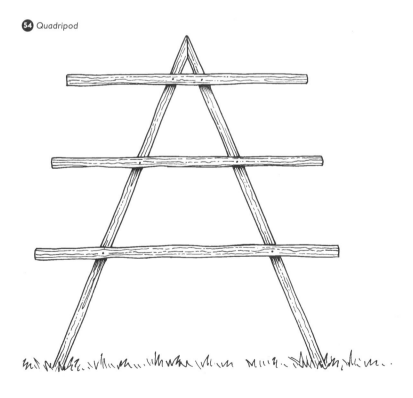

54 Quadripod

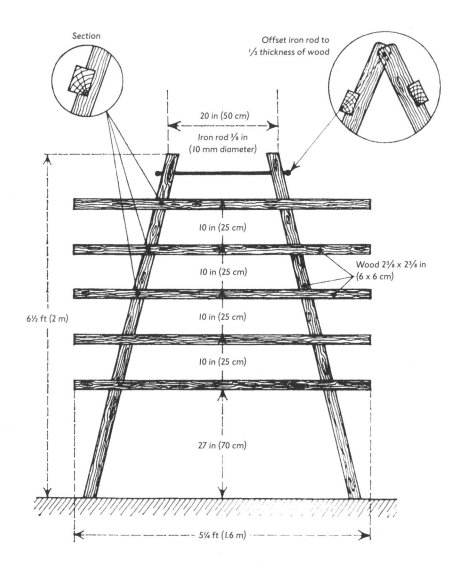

55 Alternative quadripod

Section

Offset iron rod to
⅓ thickness of wood

20 in (50 cm)

Iron rod ⅜ in
(10 mm diameter)

10 in (25 cm)

10 in (25 cm)

Wood 2⅜ x 2⅜ in
(6 x 6 cm)

10 in (25 cm)

6½ ft (2 m)

10 in (25 cm)

27 in (70 cm)

5¼ ft (1.6 m)

unnecessary and damaging to the hay (leaf shatter) unless it has rained so much for so long that the hay is at risk of moulding unless it is dried quickly. Before unloading, be absolutely sure that even the innermost hay is completely dry. Unload quadripods in the field directly into the wagon or cart, or simply flip upside down to transfer the grass to the ground to be loaded into the transport with a fork.

PROS Made mostly of wood; construction does not require a lot of skill; once it is built, it is always there and can be pulled out whenever necessary; can be used even on thin, stony soils (does not need to be pounded into the ground); when loaded properly, air circulates well, encouraging fast, even drying; can be used to dry sheaves of small grains.

CONS When overloaded, hay in the cap and along the bottom crossbar is likely to mould; difficult to transport to and from field; lots of space required for storage.

SWEDISH WIRE RACK AND BAR RACK

CONSTRUCTION Traditionally, Swedish wire racks were made with 6 ft (1.8 m) long posts with 4–5 notches and a point at the bottom. The bottom notch is made a bit over 3¼ ft (1 m), the rest of the notches are about 1¼ ft (38 cm) apart, with the top notch being 2–4 in (5–10 cm) below the top of the post. Galvanized iron wire 3mm in diameter forms the racks between the posts. Metal T-posts should also make effective wire racks.

Dimensions for Swedish bar racks are the same as for wire racks, the only difference being that instead of wire, lathe or wooden crossbars are used, held up by diagonal dowels or nails.

NUMBER REQUIRED PER ACRE (HECTARE) WIRE About 100 (250) posts and 3200 ft /975 m (13000 ft/3960 m) of wire, plus anchoring material (stakes, chains, hooks and rings). Bar: 80–120 (200–300) 4 yd (3.6 m) long racks.

INSTALLATION IN THE FIELD AND LOADING WIRE First determine the general orientation, number and length of racks. Orient the racks so that prevailing winds blow along their length ('along the wall, not into the wall') for maximum stability. Situate racks 11–16½ yd (10–15 m) apart – the higher the yield of grass, the farther apart. Depending on the size and shape of the field, racks are typically 33–55 yd (30–50 m) long.

Each rack requires a good 18 in (45 cm) of ground free of mown grass. With a post-hole digging bar, make a hole 12–16 in (30–40 cm) deep every 4¼–5½ yd (4–5 m). If the posts used are short enough, they can be pounded into the ground with a sledgehammer without making holes. At the beginning and end of every rack, drive a stake or T-post diagonally into the ground as an anchor.

To set up the wire, use a hook to attach one end of the wire to a ring on the anchor and to a chain on the other anchor. Thread wire into each notch on the poles starting with the bottom and ensure it is tight enough that it does not sag. Before adding the next wire, load the first wire with grass all the way down. With two people, one person can load from each side. If the grass has been dried somewhat, load more on the wire; if freshly cut, load less. When the first wire is full, set up the next wire and so on. Cap each post with more hay so rain cannot travel down the post. For extra support during strong winds, lean support posts into the vertical posts of the rack on each side.

BAR Proceed in the same way, but load grass around the crossbar supports to help lock the crossbars in place. Racks can also be set up in a zig-zag pattern for extra stability.

UNLOADING WIRE Grass should remain on the wire racks until it is dry enough for storage. Remove from the rack either directly into the wagon or cart or make a windrow on the ground to be picked up with a hayfork.

BAR Easiest with two people. Each person takes an end of a crossbar and the hay is tossed to the ground.

PROS Swedish racks can handle freshly cut dewy and rain-soaked grass; this is the only kind of rack that allows you to mow and make hay during prolonged periods of rain.

CONS Long set-up time.

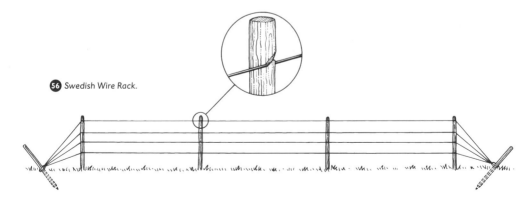

56 Swedish Wire Rack.

Which Method to Use

There is no hay-curing technique that is ideal for every situation – each has its strengths and weaknesses. Your requirements in your specific situation will dictate your choices. The chart below summarizes some of the advantages and disadvantages of the various techniques discussed in this book (adapted from Geith's *Die sichere Heuernte*).

At first glance, Swedish racks appear to be the type that can do it all: they can be hung with rain-soaked grass, respiration losses are kept to a minimum through quick drying, leaf shatter is kept to a minimum because the hay is never tedded, washout is kept to a minimum by lapped, layered stacking and good air circulation minimizes losses due to fermentation, overheating and mould

growth. Yet Swedish racks also represent potentially the costliest and most labour-intensive method. If you had access to free wood (your own timber or recycled boards), plenty of storage space and an easy-enough way of getting quadripods to and from the field, you would have almost all the advantages of Swedish racks without having to build the racks anew every time you made hay. If you had access to free wood but little storage space, you could generally use Tyrolean poles, but if rainy weather is delaying mowing, you could switch to Swedish racks. In any case, you may find it beneficial to try out various methods so that you can arrange to have flexibility under changing weather conditions.

Curing Technique	Can Start Mowing in Rainy Weather?	Respiration Losses	Leaf Shatter Risk	Washout Risk in Long Periods of Rain	Fermentation/ Overheating Losses	Risk of Mould Growth in Long Periods of Rain
Ground	No	Yes	High	Medium if windrowing done in time, high if not	Low in ideal weather, high in poor weather	High
Basic Pole	Yes	Minimal	Low	Medium	Low in ideal weather, high in poor weather	High
Tyrolean Pole	No	Minimal	Low	Low	Low	Medium
Quadripod	Yes, if racks are lightly loaded	Minimal	Low	Low	Low	Low when lightly packed, high when too densely packed
Swedish Rack	Yes	Minimal	Low	Low	Low	Low

When to Begin Hay-making

Nutritional content, digestibility and yield of the hay harvest are all dependent upon the timing of hay-making. Earlier harvests make for hay with higher digestible-protein contents, while later ones bring a larger quantity of hay. It is easy to confuse the quantity of hay with the quality and quantity of digestible nutrients contained therein. In other words, a haymow full of late-harvested, nutrient-poor hay that does not whet your animals' appetites probably contributes fewer digestible nutrients to their diet than a half-full haymow of younger-harvested, nutrient-rich hay. As soon as the flowers of grasses have withered and seeds begin to mature, plants begin to lignify, the proportion of raw fibre in the plants rises and digestibility goes down. The more an animal's body needs to work at digestion, the less the feed ultimately contributes to health and production.

This emphasizes the need to break dependence upon the weather to produce winter fodder of the highest possible quality. If your operation is set up so that you can only make hay when the weather is ideal, there will be some times when you can get away with it and bring in a decent hay crop and others when you have to wait so long that the amount of digestible nutrients in the hay is reduced by a third or more. Over time your overall winter forage quality will be poorer than if you used racks to make hay when it is raining.

If we forget about the weather for a moment, though, and consider only the plants, the ideal time to mow is when the most important grasses begin to flower, these being the ones that make up the bulk of the nutrition of the hay. It is the nutrition of these that you want to maximize. But, if you are a small operation, perhaps with only one person doing all the mowing, the hay harvest may take place over a period of 2–3 weeks, or perhaps even continuously throughout the growing season. In this case, start harvesting before the most important grasses start to bloom, so that on average forage will have been cut around the beginning of flowering, some a bit earlier, some perhaps a bit later. In any case, take advantage of every period of hay-making weather that you can, even when it seems too early and even if your neighbours haven't started mowing yet. Early harvests may yield less, but the resultant winter forage will be highly nutritious. An early first cut also makes for better-yielding second and third cuts (or makes third cuts possible at all) and prevents some weed plants from going to seed.

Make observations when you are hay-making to help you with timing your mowing. Perhaps wild plums or some other plant are in bloom at the ideal time to mow for you. Though different plants will react to climatic changes in different ways, in time you will notice the relationships between the life stages of wild plants and of your cultivated plants and you can use these to help with decisions about timing.

Above all, come up with your own schedule for hay-making. Odds are, you will be the only one in your area making hay by hand so looking to when other farmers in the area are making hay will not be helpful. It is highly likely you will want to start making hay before those using machines start to make theirs.

*A meadow of fully-loaded quadripods,
all oriented such that prevailing winds can
pass through their openings.*

*Swedish bar racks, set up at right angles to one
another, look like walls of hay in the field.*

Grass growth and the S-Curve

Another important factor to consider when deciding when to mow is the S-shaped growth curve for grass plants (and for all organisms). When the plants making up a meadow are cut, their initial regrowth is not directly powered by photosynthesis, but instead by energy and nutrients stored at the base of the stalks and in the roots. The latter die off as the plant sends out new shoots to form green leaves that can photosynthesize and fuel more new growth. Until photosynthesis restarts, growth is slow. Once leaf surface area reaches critical mass, however, growth accelerates until the plant is mature enough to divert energy from growth into reproduction (flowering and seed production).

When grass is harvested just before flowering, the plant's growth has had a maximum period of rapid growth and the plant is returned to the beginning of the growth cycle. Since harvesting on this schedule means that meadow plants spend more of their lives in a period of rapid growth, this increases the overall yield possible than if grass were generally harvested before or after the 'elbow' of the S-curve.

In continental climates, grass growth is most rapid in the spring. As summer's heat increases, grass growth generally decelerates as individual plants wither in the midday heat to conserve water. This means that the time between grass harvests will increase as the growing season progresses. Insufficient rest periods lead to smaller quantities of less-nourishing grass.

As André Voisin states in *Grass Productivity*: 'Young grass, cut every week:

1 Is very rich in crude protein.
2 Contains very little crude fibre and ballast
3 Is relatively rich in potassium and phosphorus and relatively poor in calcium.
4 The nutritive ratio (ratio of digestible crude protein to starch equivalent) is very narrow; that is to say, the proportion of protein . . . is much too high in relation to the nutritive units.'

When practising rational or holistic grazing, make hay in paddocks taken out of rotation in the early part of the growing season when grass growth is most rapid. Under such grazing systems, more paddocks are required as the growing season progresses to observe increasing rest periods. Since rest periods are short at the beginning of the growing season, not all paddocks can be grazed, but must instead be mown so that the rest period is not excessive when they are later grazed. Take advantage of this by making hay from these mown pastures. Be sure not to take the same paddocks out of the grazing rotation in consecutive years to maintain floral diversity and high yields.

As Ernst Klapp wrote in *Wiesen und Weiden* in 1954,'The first essential of economic pasture management is to remember that the flora of a pasture is extremely plastic and varies very rapidly with the management applied.' Klapp demonstrated that the number of annual cuts influences the composition of the flora, as in the table featured below which demonstrates that increasing the number of annual cuts reduces the yield of meadow fescue far more than it reduces the yield of white clover (adapted from Voisin, 1959).

Experiments by Professor Johnstone-Wallace in the 1940s in sown fields of Kentucky blue grass and white clover showed that the percentage of white clover in the field can vary from 1 per cent to 80 per cent, depending on the management employed.

English name	Latin name	Relative yield at 2–3 cuts per year	Relative yield at 4-6 cuts per year	Relative yield at 7-13 cuts per year
White clover	*Trifolium repens*	100	64	58
Kentucky blue grass	*Poa pratensis*	100	96	35
Perennial rye-grass	*Lolium perenne*	100	68	31
Cocksfoot	*Dactylis*	100	67	31
Red fescue	*Festuca rubra*	100	65	25
Meadow fescue	*Festuca pratensis*	100	57	18
Marsh poa	*Poa palustris*	100	19	8

Making the Best
Ground-cured Hay

When the weather is sunny and dry allowing for curing in three days, and you are relaxed about the possibility that the weather forecast is wrong, and you do not mind concentrating the entire first cut into a day or two, it is hard to recommend bringing out the racks even if they help reduce the risk of leaf shatter. When all other conditions are perfect, using racks does indeed bring extra work and only relatively small benefit.

There are diverse opinions about windrowing the hay for overnight and tedding again the next day. It is extra work and, especially on the last day, will probably lead to increased incidence of leaf shatter, so it can be tempting to just ted once after mowing and to leave it as is until bringing the hay in. Be aware of the following advantages to overnight windrowing before making your decision:

+ You get most of the grass up off the ground, helping to create a capillary break against climbing soil moisture.

+ Windrowed grass is better protected from washout from unexpected rains.

+ Morning dew forms only on the surface of the windrow, meaning the bulk of the grass starts the morning free of dew, making for faster, more even drying.

+ The ground dries faster in the morning.

+ Grass ferments lightly in windrows at night, making it slightly warmer and leading to faster drying times.

+ Turning of the grass happens automatically when re-tedding after windrowing, which helps grass dry more evenly.

Weigh these advantages against the increased workload and risk of increased nutrient losses due to leaf shatter. Remember that windrowing is only protection against brief periods of rain. If a big, unexpected storm comes, bring out the racks.

Getting the Most Out
of Hay Racks

Any time it is uncertain whether there is enough time before the next rain for your hay to dry (which, depending on local conditions, may be rare or almost always), you will need to use hay racks to protect the harvest from nutrient losses, whether directly through washout or indirectly through leaf shatter, fermentation or moulding.

Racking is your first and best defence against having to wait to begin mowing and having rain ruin what you have already cut. It is basically a vastly improved version of windrowing that allows for the curing of quality, usable winter forage even in the rain. Racking is indeed an extra step, but I for one am thankful that there is a step that can be taken. What good is it to start hay-making a week or two late, curing on the ground for 'less work', only to harvest fibre-rich, protein-poor forage that your animals hardly eat? The valuable nutrients saved by racking more than makes up for the extra effort involved. And if you make racking your standard practice, you will cease to see it as an extra step and consistently harvest the best winter forage possible.

Always cure leafy forage, such as clover or alfalfa hay, on racks, as it is highly susceptible to leaf shatter. Early first harvests and late third harvests should also always be dried on racks, as the sun will be lower and the weather will probably be too cool to dry the grass on the ground before it starts to mould. In regions with almost daily rainfall, where hay-making might be otherwise impossible, racks are a must if you want your own winter forage.

The use of hay-drying poles is what makes hay-making possible on east- and north-facing mountain slopes in the Alps.

CHAPTER 9

GROWING AND HARVESTING SMALL GRAINS

Unlike making hay, growing grains without big machines can be an exhausting, discouraging, tedious experience. Every year you prepare a seedbed and sow the seed. When the crop is ripe, you cut the tillers (stalks) with a scythe or sickle, bundle it into sheaves, then stack it to dry. You then have to thresh the grains from the ears, either with a flail or some kind of drum thresher. This threshed grain will be full of chaff and other impurities, so you winnow it. If it is a hulled grain, you will have to hull it before eating it. So why do it?

It wasn't until I had actually done all this that I understood that I no longer wanted to raise enough grains by hand to make bread on a big enough scale to earn a living. However, each step in the process, with the right attitude, can be very enjoyable in moderation. You may decide that raising enough grain to feed the family is no longer moderation, however, when you see how much is involved with each step of the process.

Still, when you consider that almost all of what most of us grow in our vegetable gardens is for condiments and side dishes that do not supply the bulk of our calories, making the jump to growing your own grains for bread, homebrew, chicken feed/bedding and compost pile fodder can be a real game-changer in terms of food autonomy, economic independence and ecological responsibility. In double-dug bio-intensive beds, yields can be as high as 24 lb (11 kg) per 100 sq ft (9 sq m), meaning that you can grow enough for about 1½ lb (700 g) of bread a week for a year (1 lb/450 g grain makes for 1½ lb/700 g bread) in 200 sq ft (18.5 sq m).

What to Grow?

Different grains have their own sets of health benefits and drawbacks, needs (environmental and agricultural) and other properties that you will want to consider before you decide what to grow. You need to know if the crop in question will contribute to your and/or your livestock's nutrition in the way that you want, if it will grow where you live, and what you must do to grow and harvest it.

There are two different types of grains: winter and spring. Winter grains are essentially biennials in that they are planted in the late summer/early autumn of the first year, grow enough to establish themselves, are dormant throughout the winter, then go to seed the following year. Though the growing seasons of two consecutive calendar years are involved, the entire life cycle takes less than 12 months. Their sowing time is advantageous because disturbing the soil that late in the season disrupts weed life cycles. Furthermore, weeds that do sprout after sowing are typically killed by winter weather, meaning that your winter grain crop – whose roots have already established dominance in the soil and whose leaves have already covered a large percentage of the ground and thus can take most advantage of sunlight – already has a huge head start against weeds in spring.

Spring grains, on the other hand, are planted and harvested during the same calendar year. Weeds have a better chance of establishing themselves in a spring grain crop because there's little opportunity to take advantage of weed life cycle disruption and winter kill. (The only way to do this would be to till the soil late the year before and 'solarize' the plot by leaving it to allow weed seeds to sprout and then die. Unfortunately, the losses to soil organic matter and the increased potential for erosion by leaving tilled, unplanted soil to overwinter cancel out whatever advantages in weed control you may gain.) Spring grains are generally harder to grow by hand than are winter grains, but they are certainly achievable and there are many grains that you might like to grow.

RYE Rye is the small grain for hand cultivation *par excellence*. It is an unbelievably hardy winter grain, so it takes advantage of winter killing of weeds. It grows to be really tall, 6 ft (1.8 m) or more, so it shades the ground well. Its roots secrete allelopathic chemicals that make it even more difficult for weeds to establish. It can be grown in just about any soil and is not susceptible to rust. The main disadvantage of rye – it is highly susceptible to the fungal disease ergot – is fairly easy to deal with for the small-scale grower: just remove ergot growth by hand as you thresh.

Rye is unusual among grains for the high level of fibre in its endosperm – not just in its bran. As a result, rye products generally have a lower glycaemic index than products made from wheat and most other grains, making it especially healthy for diabetics.

This crop can be grown almost anywhere, as it tolerates many different extremes of climate. It is grown in mountains and in valleys, in continental Minnesota and along the coast of Brittany. It tolerates wet, cool, cloudy climates better than wheat, yet also thrives in areas with hot, dry summers thanks to its ability to take full advantage of spring moisture with its extensive root system and the 70 atmospheres of pressure it can produce to take up water. The only soils that rye finds challenging are water-logged, poorly drained ones.

Sow rye in the garden following potatoes or other crops that are harvested early enough for rye to prevent fallow patches and make optimal use of space in the garden.

Rye should be harvested in the yellow-ripeness stage as it completes its ripening well after cutting. Waiting until full (dead) ripeness risks yield reductions due to grains falling off the ears. Ripen cut rye in stooks or on racks, ideally with a cap, which helps with ripening.

WHEAT, ANCIENT AND MODERN

Ancient wheats are more nutrient-dense than modern wheat. The latter has been so changed over the years by the selective breeding that has greatly increased its yields that it hardly resembles its ancient cousins emmer, einkorn, spelt and khorasan wheat. Though modern wheat has much higher overall yields than ancient wheats, the quality of those yields is significantly lower; the vitamins, minerals and trace minerals contents are all greatly reduced. There is even anecdotal evidence that people suffering from coeliac disease can eat emmer because it has a simpler gluten structure that is theoretically easier to digest, owing to its different ancestry from modern wheat and all other ancient wheats.

The main difficulty in growing ancient grains without machines is that they are all hulled grains, except for khorasan wheat. The hulls are tough, woody, inedible and difficult to remove without machinery. It is possible to convert a Corona-style grain mill into a grain huller (see Resources & Supplies), which I encourage you to do if you choose to grow these grains, but it represents an extra step in the process.

If you are growing an ancient wheat at the field scale (even if it is a fairly small field), khorasan wheat is probably the choice for you. As it is a spring grain you will not be able to take advantage of winter kill, so be sure to use an undersown crop to help keep weeds to a minimum. If you are growing an ancient wheat at the garden scale and are expecting a yield of 100 lb (45 kg) or less, or if you do not mind hulling more than 100 lb (45 kg) of grain, give emmer, einkorn or spelt a try.

SPELT Spelt is, along with rye, one of the hardiest grains there are. It does not yield as much as wheat in 'normal' years, but since it is hardly affected by extremes of weather, it out-yields wheat in unusually hot, cold, wet or dry years. It is also less sensitive to different soil conditions and to late plantings than wheat. In other words, spelt is extremely flexible and yields reliably well, even when growing conditions are less than ideal. Acidic and sandy soils present the biggest challenges to growing it.

Sow spelt later than winter wheat; it can even be sown into autumn if the weather allows. It has very narrow leaves, so it may at first appear that you have sown too thinly, even when you have not. As soon as growth resumes in spring, the field will fill in well, as spelt plants are very robust. Stands of spelt that are too dense are more liable to lodge (lie down) than otherwise. 'Harrow' such stands with a bow rake in the spring to help prevent lodging. If this doesn't seem to improve matters, you can even mow it as long as tillering has not yet begun, taking care to not mow too close to the ground.

Ideally you should harvest spelt no earlier than the yellow-ripeness stage, but you can also harvest it in full (dead) ripeness. Harvested in full ripeness, it can often be brought in the same day, as spelt dries very quickly. When dry weather prevails around harvest time, ears can break off during harvest, so harvest earlier in dry years to help prevent this. When harvesting for Grünkern, a mineral-rich young-harvested form of the grain used in soups in the German-speaking world, harvest in the early milk-ripe stage and dry fully before hulling.

OATS Hulled grains make for one more step in the cultivation process and, especially when growing by hand, it is best to eliminate a step any time you can. 'Naked oats' have been bred to have a minuscule to non-existent hull, so that they thresh clean, needing only winnowing to be ready for culinary use.

Oats are another grain that does well in almost any soil and in diverse climates. The most critical factor in getting a decent oat harvest is the oats getting sufficient water, which is particularly challenging in sandier soils and those with higher lime content. Oats do especially well in cool, moist weather; where it is too wet or cool to cultivate other grains, you can probably grow oats. The lower the temperature during tillering, the higher the yield. Oats like lots of iron, manganese and phosphorous, metabolize nitrogen well and are sensitive to salty soils.

Grow oats after anything, even other grass-family crops, except a previous crop of oats. They tolerate acid as well as alkaline soils and do well in humus-rich, high-nitrogen soils, making them an ideal crop to grow when using animal impact (see p. 120) to prepare a seed bed.

Oats can be sown even when soils are fairly waterlogged and actually seem to prefer wet soils for sowing. In any case, they require plenty of water after sowing, which means that mulching the seed bed lightly is especially useful. Seeding rate can vary quite a bit from one variety to another, as some grow into narrow plants that take up little space while others are robust plants with long horizontal growth that requires more space and, hence, a thinner seeding rate.

Harvest oats in the yellow-ripe phase, being careful to not harvest too late, which risks knocking seeds to the ground. The straw will still contain much water at this point, so it is especially important to dry cut oats on a rack as they will need a long time to dry, at least 10–14 days. Again, the danger of bringing oats in too early is greatest in hot, dry weather, because it is easy to get the impression from the outside of the grains that they are dry, but in reality they are still wet on the inside.

BARLEY Barley (contains gluten) is probably most useful for making malt for brewing beer. Interest in craft beers and homebrewing seems to grow every year. The ultimate craft brew would have to be beer made from barley that you have grown yourself. Standard varieties of barley yield hulled grains, but naked-seed varieties would probably best suit the home-scale grower. Although the seeds of naked barley varieties are encased in hulls on the ear, the seeds are not attached to them and thus thresh more or less as easily as wheat and rye. Experiment with different varieties, crop rotations and growing conditions to create your own unique homebrews.

Grow Your Own Porridge?

You may be tempted to grow oats for your own morning porridge. While it is not impossible to do at home, making rolled oats as we know them today is not straightforward as they are the result of fairly extensive industrial processing. The oats, commercial varieties of which are hulled grains, are hulled by shooting them against a wall at an exactly calibrated speed, which causes the hull to break off without cracking the grain.

The hulled grains ('groats') are then roasted because the hulling causes part of the germ to be exposed to air, which would oxidize the oils contained therein. Roasting stabilizes these oils despite their exposure to air. Groats are then steamed before rolling so that their starchy innards do not pulverize into flour.

Oats are a gluten-free grain, but many with coeliac disease avoid them anyway for two reasons. For one, oats from the store are often processed with equipment that also handles gluten-containing grains, which then contaminates the oats. Additionally, oats contain a gluten-like protein called avenin, which some with coeliac disease may not tolerate, thus rendering for them even home-grown oats out of the question.

Growing for Thatch

Rye is the classic grain for thatching material because of its long stalks and resistance to rust. Winter wheat that has not been bred for shortened tillers (especially the ancient wheats and older strains of modern wheat such as Maris Huntsman and Maris Widgeon) also makes for excellent thatch in that the stalks are sufficiently long (2½–4 ft [76–120 cm]) and their centres are not spongy. Oats, barley and spring wheat are the grains of last resort. Harvesting a bit greener than usual makes for sheaves that are less brittle and thus not as easily damaged during handling.

The ideal straw for thatching is described in Jacqueline Fearn's *Thatch and Thatching*: 'The best straw comes from winter wheat on moderate to heavy soils with little use of artificial fertiliser and agrochemicals (to minimise the nitrate levels) . . . . It is reaped before it is fully ripe, then bound and [stooked] for about two weeks, allowing the heads to ripen without taking strength from the straw. After further ripening in a corn stack the wheat is threshed according to its future use as combed wheat reed or long straw.'

Dealing with Weeds

When growing grains without machines, there are a few aspects you will want to take full advantage of to deal with weeds. They are solarization, undersowing a companion crop and winter kill.

Solarization is simple. It essentially amounts to preparing the seed bed twice in that you plough the soil or 'plough' with chickens or pigs and then do nothing with the prepared area for a week or two. This allows weed seeds time to sprout and grow a bit. Then, send the animals back to clear the vegetation another time before sowing the grain seed. This has the effect of depleting the weed seed bank and potentially reducing weed pressure with your crop.

Undersowing is the practice of sowing seeds of plants other than the main crop before, at the same time or after sowing crop seeds so that these companion plants grow in the understorey of the main crop. They are selected for their benignity or neutrality towards the main crop and their presence in the understorey – taking in any light that makes it past the main crop and occupying root space that the main crop does not – make it that much more difficult for any weeds to establish.

Taking advantage of the winter killing of some weeds essentially means growing winter grains. These are planted in autumn and grow enough to establish themselves and survive the winter. Many weeds that start to grow in autumn will not be as hardy as the winter grain and will be killed by freezing temperatures over the winter. When spring comes and the winter grain begins to grow again, the number of weeds in the field will have been reduced and the grain will have a big head start on anything that may sprout after winter.

Some more factors that help with weed control are crop rotation, getting your crop sown on time, sowing the right amount of seed and distributing it evenly. Crop rotation may be one of the most crucial things you can do to control weeds when growing grains without machines, though this is perhaps

Preparing a Seed Bed

more realistic in the garden, where weeds are in any case easier to manage. For field-scale cultivation, the most important thing is to not grow grain year after year in the same field. All other measures to minimize weeds being equal, weeds will steadily increase as they adapt to the cultivation methods and the properties of the crops themselves. They germinate under the same conditions, react the same to various climatic conditions and utilize the same nutrients.

In rotating crops at the field scale, the two main options are to rotate the location of the field taken out of pasture to grow small grains or to keep the location constant but rotate the crop(s) grown within. When choosing the former option, you can take advantage of the fertility built up in the soil after years of grazing and manuring (though rye and wheat do better without so much nitrogen; oats are probably the best small grain for this situation).

The latter option of keeping the field location constant has the potential advantage of any ideal properties of the location, such as proximity to buildings, solar exposure or soil fertility. With a fixed field, keeping an ideal crop rotation may require that you grow several years' supply of the given crop each year. For example, you might grow a three-year supply of corn the first year, a three-year supply of oats the second year and a three-year supply of rye the third year, before starting the rotation over the fourth year. You might choose to do it this way with a 'mobile' field as well, or grow one-year supplies of all your field crops in that patch before moving on the following year.

Grains, legumes and all other seeds require a medium in which to grow and from which to draw the nutrients and water required for life, as well as the right temperature and time to germinate.

Ploughing and dragging a field makes no ecological, economic or moral sense at the homestead scale and smaller. All that equipment needs someone to purchase it, maintain it, operate it, store it and quench its thirst for fuel. In return, while helping you work the fields, it also compacts the soil, turns the air into poison gas, kills flora and fauna in the ground (directly by driving over them and somewhat less directly by disturbing the soil with the plough), makes a lot of noise and generally turns your attention from thinking about the land to thinking about machines.

Additionally, turning the soil is about the worst thing you could possibly do to it. Different kinds of micro-organisms, be they bacteria or fungi, thrive at different soil depths. Digging into the soil and flipping it over does indeed clear the soil surface of vegetation, which is what is required for a seed bed, but it also has the effect of mixing subsoil with topsoil. The former surface vegetation then decomposes anaerobically (that is, it rots), topsoil and subsoil micro-organisms die because they are no longer experiencing the conditions they require to live and overall soil organic matter levels decrease, leaving behind a soil where grain seeds can sprout but are then stuck in a growing medium of increasingly poor quality.

The ideally prepared seed bed has soil layers that are still intact, yet are still aerated enough for roots to grow through them and for those roots to find the air, water and nutrients they need. The two main methods that accomplish all this are bio-intensive gardening and animal impact.

The former essentially involves double-digging garden beds and the use of copious amounts of nutrient-dense compost. Double-digging is a process whereby the existing soil profile is maintained as topsoil and subsoil are dug separately. Garden beds are aerated about twice as deep when double-dug than when single-dug. This, combined with adding compost to the topsoil layer, allows for much higher seeding rates and greatly increased yields per unit of land. With the yields stated by Jon Jeavons in *How to Grow More Vegetables*, you can grow all of the small grains you need every year, without ever having to take grassland out of rotation, by just growing a garden bed or two of small grains.

If you want to grow more small grains than you will consume, perhaps because you want to bake bread for sale or put a bit of fat on your otherwise pasture-fed livestock before slaughter, double-digging the required number of beds may end up being more work than you are willing to do. In this case, use animal impact to prepare additional beds or a field. Animals such as chickens or pigs, when kept in place for days or weeks, will remove vegetation from the surface of the soil, fertilize the topsoil with their manure, disturb the soil's surface enough to provide aeration (animals left too long will then compact the soil, however), yet at the same time not disturb deeper soil levels, leaving the soil's natural aeration – provided by plant roots, worms and such – intact.

When using chickens for soil preparation, moveable coops called chicken tractors are cheap, effective and easy ways to keep chickens in one place long enough for them to clear the ground, scratch it up and manure it. Once the chickens have improved the bed to your satisfaction, move them along and sow seed by broadcasting. If the topsoil is compacted, loosen it with a garden fork to a depth of about 1 in (2.5 cm) by sticking it in the ground here and there and wiggling it a bit. Cover seeds lightly with compost and mulch very lightly with straw to help with water retention. Press everything down slightly to improve seed-to-soil contact with either a garden roller or a hay rake.

Pigs, in addition to clearing the soil's surface of vegetation and manuring, will root into the ground and loosen the surface of the soil. Getting them to stay in the desired plot can be challenging, but portable electric fencing can be very effective to this end. Just be sure to provide them with some shelter from the elements, perhaps by constructing a mobile pen if you are moving them frequently and/or far. To get them to dig even more or to clear large tree roots, sprinkle maize kernels as needed.

Small-scale Seed Sowing

Mechanical seeders (seed 'drills') work by opening up dozens of furrows per pass, dropping seed into them at a prescribed rate, then covering them. There are small human-powered seed drills that are used by market gardeners to directly sow large-garden amounts of seeds for crops such as sweet corn and sugar snap peas that can be set up

A small, hand-cranked seed broadcaster.

for efficiently sowing seed for small grains. At scales beyond the garden scale up to, say, ½ acre (0.2 ha), these human-powered drills can be a sensible option for sowing seed as they can ensure even coverage and bury the seed, thus maximizing soil contact and helping to protect the seed from birds.

However, unless you are committed to growing beyond the garden scale every year, simply broadcasting seed is an effective enough method for sowing grain. Calculate the amount of seed you will need for the area required beforehand and have this measured out as you begin so you can monitor how much seed you are using as a percentage of the total needed and adjust seed density as needed.

Broadcasting seed means tossing the seed on the ground in such a way that it is spread evenly at the required density. This can be done by hand by tossing seed held in the fist in a side-arm motion, using a finger to help the seed spray out and land over a larger area. Easier and more effective are small, hand-cranked seed broadcasters. You simply pour seed in a hopper, turn a crank and walk across the field as the seed sprays out over the ground. Press seed into the soil by walking across the field and pressing down with a hay rake in front of you or by rolling with a garden roller. Cover very lightly with straw to allow plenty of light to strike the soil's surface, yet still help with water retention.

Harvesting

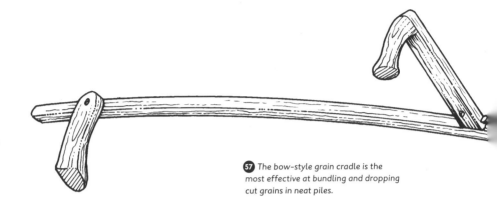

57 *The bow-style grain cradle is the most effective at bundling and dropping cut grains in neat piles.*

The timing of the harvest is critical in determining whether the grains you harvest will ripen properly and whether you will have significant losses due to grains falling off the ears during harvesting. To ensure that grains are sufficiently developed, wait until the so-called yellow-ripeness phase to cut. The yellow ripeness is characterized by full, bulbous grains that break (rather than get squashed) when squeezed with a fingernail, yet are still somewhat soft. The contents of the grains are no longer milky, but rather have become tough, somewhat dry and perhaps even a bit translucent. The leaves have begun to die off and most (but not necessarily all) of the stalk has turned yellow.

The longer you wait after plants have reached yellow-ripeness, the greater the danger of losing grains from the ears as you harvest. Oats, rye, spelt and certain loose-eared spring wheat varieties present the greatest risk of grain fall-out, whereas other wheat varieties (especially those with plump ears such as khorasan wheat) and barley present the least risk and should even be harvested at full (dead) ripeness for maximum nutritional content. In other words, be sure not to harvest oats and rye too late and wheat and barley too soon. An additional disadvantage of waiting until full ripeness to harvest is that as soon as the plant dies, weeds suddenly begin to thrive because of reduced competition. Having all that extra green material in your sheaves of grain is a major inconvenience at least and at worst a cause for mould growth that can reduce the storage life of your crop.

REAPING WITH OR WITHOUT A GRAIN CRADLE For many centuries, small grains have been harvested with a sickle, a one-handed tool that allows for the bundling of stalks with the left hand and cutting with the right. This technique has the advantage that bundles can be left neatly in the field for easy binding.

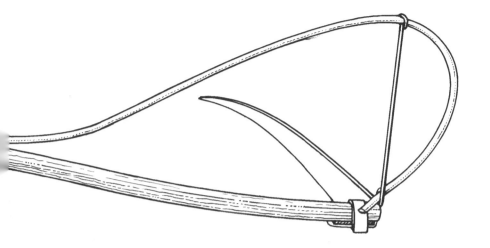

The disadvantage of using a sickle, however, is that you are constantly squatting or stooping near the ground. Some techniques for doing this are better than others, but for most of us it is hugely taxing and painful to harvest with a sickle for more than a few minutes.

The scythe was originally invented to harvest grass, but eventually it was also employed in the harvesting of small grains. It has the huge advantage of making mowing in an upright position possible. There are two main concerns in using the scythe to harvest small grains. One is blade maintenance. For harvesting tender grass, it is advantageous to peen the blade to maximum sharpness (that is, thinness). But the woody stalks of small grains are anything but tender and, though the blade must be sharp, it must be peened so that the cutting edge is robust enough to cut through tough stalks yet still retains its shape and does not become damaged.

When peening the blade you use to harvest small grains (a dedicated blade will make your life easier), make the bevelled edge narrower (less drawn out) than when peening for grass. In practical terms, this typically means peening in two passes – one to bring material down, one to compress/harden – rather than three. When testing the thinness of the edge with your fingernail, a blade peened for harvesting small grains will not give at all.

Because the cutting edge is shorter and more robust when peened in this way, a fine natural whetstone for honing will no longer suffice, as such stones simply reshape the material of the microscopic outer cutting edge and remove practically no material. Choose instead a coarse natural stone or a fine artificial stone – depending on the robustness of the edge – that wears away a small amount of the cutting edge and is what is required here to keep the blade sharp.

58 *First stroke cuts stalks. Stalks fall to mower's right at spot of cut leaving stalks splayed across mowing semi-circle.*

The other main concern when using a scythe to harvest small grains is ensuring that the cut grain lies in the field in such a way that it can easily be bound. The most well-known solution to this is attaching a so-called cradle to the scythe. There are many different designs, but the most effective is

one that prevents grain from falling back in the direction the scythe is coming from (to the right as you mow), collects it, and allows it to fall to the left in untangled bunches **57**. A lesser-known technique is to have a person standing slightly ahead of the mower who uses a stick to prevent the grains from falling

59 *Second stroke at same spot (without advancing) gathers stalks together into one bundle and flips them over before depositing this neat bundle to the mower's left.*

to the right. The mower with both of these techniques typically mows 'into the wall', that is, into standing grain. A third technique is to mow 'away from the wall' and mow in two strokes. The first stroke cuts the grain, which in this case does indeed fall to the right **58** with the stalks splayed across the mowing circle. A second stroke in the same place gathers the cut grain into a bundle and flips the stalks over before delivering them to the left **59** . This requires twice as many strokes to cut the grain, but requires neither tinkering with the scythe nor an extra person.

Curing the Cut Grain

Harvest during a dry period if at all possible to ensure that water can slowly and thoroughly exit grains and straw, which contributes to better ripening (which completes after cutting). Rain during or just before the harvest can cause nutrient leaching and influence the colour, fragrance, viability and brewing/baking qualities of the grain.

Protect grains from precipitation and ground moisture by standing up sheaves of grain into stooks – ideally capped by a sheaf of grain or a cloth – or, even more effective and easier than making capped stooks, by hanging the grain up on quadripod hayracks. The ears should be oriented towards the inside of the quadripod; in this way you can leave grain outside in the rain for weeks at a time if necessary. Getting cut grain off the ground ensures a slow, even progression of the grain to full ripeness. Too-rapid, uneven ripening can lead to shrinking of the grains and rotting.

Be sure that the grains are fully dried before bringing them in from the field. This prevents their heating up in storage, which may have an effect on colour, fragrance and viability. Bringing grain in too early is almost a greater danger in hot, dry summers as in cool, wet ones in that grain that dries too quickly may seem dry enough, but in reality it is only the outer layer that is so dry.

Grain is ready to harvest when it reaches yellow-ripeness phase.

Directly Harvesting with Livestock

Some or all of your stand of small grains (or flaxseed, legumes and so on) can be harvested directly by livestock. The most effective method in terms of completeness of harvesting, tillage and eliminating any harvesting or processing is to first turn the plot over to chickens for harvesting the seed and then following with pigs to turn the straw and other dry matter into the soil.

Another possibility that reduces the amount of harvesting work involved is to harvest only part of your plot and turn the rest over to the chickens and pigs. You can also take care of bedding and feeding in one fell swoop by reaping, binding and bringing in the harvest, but then using the unthreshed sheaves as bedding and allowing chickens to peck out the seeds.

Allowing livestock to directly harvest seed crops has the disadvantage of not allowing for milling. But when left outside for long enough or by soaking the ears before tossing to the chickens, seeds may sprout on their own to a certain degree, making for a more nutritious and digestible feed.

Threshing and Winnowing

Threshing is the process of separating the seed from the ear. Classically this was done by striking a pile of cut stalks with a flail on a large sheet. Eventually, powered machines (first powered by horses on treadmills, later by diesel) took this over, using either a rotating drum with spikes sticking out to knock the grains off the ears or passing the grain between two belts moving at different speeds that rubbed the grain off. A modern, low-tech yet highly effective method of threshing is to staple a piece of welded metal mesh to a board, place the ears on it, then step on them to rub them across the mesh.

After threshing, grain is winnowed –

cleaned by separating the seed from the chaff (dried plant debris). Chaff is much lighter than starchy seeds and will blow away in the wind. So, pouring from bucket to bucket with a fan nearby is an easy method. Various seed-cleaning machines blow air past grains as they fall from hopper to hopper inside the machine. These are effective and convenient, but can be quite expensive.

An ingenious treadle-powered drum thresher **60** is the ultimate human-powered tool for threshing. It is not a particularly cheap piece of equipment, but it is an elegant and effective solution for those wanting to grow something like 1 acre (0.4 ha) of small grains. A few years ago, I had a friend build a pedal-powered drum thresher out of a wooden cable spool and an old bicycle on a pallet, which was not as effective as I had hoped it would be (because of my design, not my friend's building abilities!) A design with bearings or some other way to reduce friction, plus a barrier to deflect threshed seeds, would have been much more effective.

60 Treadle-powered drum thresher. Can also be built with an old wooden cable spool connected to a bicycle (see page 129).

Storage

The grains are of course seeds and for them to remain viable and edible for long periods of time, they need to be treated as such. Before they even go into storage, they need to have a moisture content that is low enough to prevent fermentation and mould formation.

Seeds need two things to germinate: water and a certain temperature range. By denying them these things, you prevent them from germinating, so store grains in a cool, dry place.

Ricks are stacks of unthreshed sheaves that are kept off the ground by a table-like framework. This serves the dual purposes of keeping the grain away from rising damp from the ground and, when mouse-guards are employed, protecting it from pests.

Constructing ricks and making sure they stay dry and pest-free is potentially a lot of labour, but if you are able to make them work for you, they have the advantage of allowing you to thresh and winnow on an as-needed basis instead of doing it all at once, which can be a huge undertaking if you have grown an acre (0.4 ha) or more of small grains.

Processing

Whole grains can be extremely nutritious for humans, but an oft-overlooked requirement for this to be so is their proper preparation. Grains in general and wheat in particular have high glycaemic indexes (that is, their consumption causes a high spike in blood sugar levels) when eaten as they typically are in our modern society: ground, leavened with yeast and baked. Additionally, whole grains (indeed all seeds) contain stored phosphorous in the form of phytic acid in

their brans. Phytic acid is not toxic, but it is not digestible by humans and it bonds readily with calcium, magnesium and other minerals. This phenomenon prevents the uptake of these nutrients in meals containing foods with phytic acid. Fortunately there are ways to reduce the glycaemic indexes of grains and to neutralize their phytic acid content: fermentation and germination.

Fermentation is an effervescent reaction brought on by micro-organisms such as bacteria and fungi (including yeast). The simplest way to achieve this with whole grains is by submerging them in water, adding an acid (for example whey, vinegar or lemon juice) and letting them soak overnight at room temperature. The anaerobic conditions provided by the water, the acid, the 'food' provided by the grains themselves and moderate temperatures provide the perfect growing conditions for lactic acid-producing bacteria and wild yeasts, which are present in the air and in whey and vinegar that have not been subjected to heat (pasteurized). Ferment for at least 8 hours or up to 24 hours to significantly break down the phytic acid content of the bran.

Sourdough is another method of fermentation, used for grains that have already been ground into flour. In its most simple form, sourdough is nothing more than flour that has been mixed with water and allowed to sit in warmth until lactic acid bacteria and wild yeasts have colonized it, causing gas bubbles and lactic acid to form, thus leavening and souring it. Add a sprinkle of salt and bake it and you have bread in its most basic form: a leavened mass of flour, salt and water that has been 'pre-digested'

A homemade, pedal-powered drum thresher uses a wooden cable spool, bike frame, pallet and some scraps.

by micro-organisms so that its anti-nutrient content and glycaemic index have been reduced to insignificant levels.

Germinating (also known as sprouting) grains and other seeds before eating them also has the effect of breaking down phytic acid and reducing their glycaemic index. Germination causes enzymes to be released that convert phytic acid into a digestible form of phosphorous and break down the starches of the endosperm. To germinate grains, soak them for 12–24 hours in a large jar, covered with a piece of muslin held in place with a rubber band. Then turn the jar upside down to drain the water and allow the water to continue to drain by placing the jar upside down in a 2-cup measuring cup or some other vessel with a mouth wider than the jar's mouth, yet narrow enough to support the jar and allow water

to drain. Rinse every 12 hours or so and drain upside down.

Grains need to soak up water to germinate but will rot in standing water, hence the draining procedure. After 2–3 days, the radicle (the tiny sprout that is the beginnings of the root system) will have emerged, at which point the grains should be used for maximum sweetness. Either grind them wet with a food processor and mix with sourdough starter to make bread or dry them in a warm oven for later grinding into flour with a grain mill.

Traditional bulgur is wheat that has been sprouted, dried and coarsely milled or 'cracked'. When you sprout, dry and mill grains finely into bulgur flour, you can use this flour to make non-sourdough-leavened recipes without worrying about anti-nutrients and a high glycaemic index.

How to Make Sourdough Bread

Whole-grain sourdough bread is the simplest, most flavourful and perhaps most nutritious bread there is. Some advice, if you are new to baking. First, use kitchen scales – measuring grain and flour by volume is highly inaccurate. Second, always use freshly ground flour, since grinding grains exposes oils in the germ to the air, which quickly oxidizes them. Finally, use fluoride-free water. In my experience, Brita-type water filters remove enough fluoride to render the water appropriate for making a sourdough starter. You can also leave tap water in an uncovered pot overnight, which allows the fluoride to evaporate.

Starter Recipe

Day 1: Mix 3½ oz (100 g) freshly ground flour with 3½ fl oz (100 ml) fluoride-free, lukewarm water (tip: 3½ fl oz (100 ml) water weighs 3½ oz (100 g), so if you don't have a measuring cup, just weigh the water) in a large bowl (ideally ceramic). Cover with a towel to keep flies out and leave to stand in a warm location (ideally 86°F/30°C) for 24 hours.

Day 2: Add 100–150 g (3½–5 oz) freshly ground flour and 3½ fl oz (100 ml) fluoride-free, lukewarm water. Stir, cover with a towel and leave to stand in a warm location for 24 hours.

Day 3: The starter should start to smell sour, which means that lactic acid is being produced because lactic acid bacteria are thriving. Add 7 oz (200 g) freshly ground flour and 7 fl oz (200 ml) fluoride-free,

lukewarm water. Stir, cover with a towel and leave to stand in a warm location (77°F/25°C) for 24 hours.

Day 4: The starter should now be sour and bubbly, with a consistency like thick pancake batter. If so, it is now ready to use, though it is not yet at full strength. Repeated use will improve its leavening power. Remove a heaped tablespoon, mix with some flour to stiffen and keep in an airtight container such as a jam jar in the refrigerator for up to two weeks, where it will keep fresh and free of mould. If you bake less often than every fortnight, you will need to refresh your starter, ideally every week or so. To do this, discard half of your saved starter, then add 2–3½ oz (50–100 g) freshly ground flour and 2–3½ fl oz (50–100 ml) fluoride-free water, mix, leave to stand in a warm location overnight, then return to the jar in the refrigerator. The cleaner your hands and the tools you use, the less likely it is that mould will develop.

Any kind of flour can be used to make a sourdough starter, as the starches from the flour, plus the water and warmth create perfect conditions for lactic acid bacteria to flourish. However, you may wish to keep a few different active starters (e.g. a rye starter and a wheat starter) if you like to bake multiple kinds of bread frequently.

Whole-Grain Sourdough Bread Recipe

This is the classic peasant farmer bread of the German-speaking world. It is a mix of mostly rye with 25 per cent wheat of some sort (wheat, spelt, khorasan wheat, emmer, einkorn). With just salt as an addition, it is already hugely flavourful and hearty. You can add one or more of several digestive herbs to give it an even fuller flavour and make it easier to digest.

Sponge
5 oz (125 g) sourdough starter
17 fl oz (500 ml) fluoride-free,
    lukewarm water
14 oz (400 g) freshly ground rye flour

Dough
1 ¾ lb (800 g) freshly ground rye flour
14 oz (400 g) freshly ground spelt, khorasan
    wheat, emmer, einkorn or wheat flour
3 heaped teaspoons unrefined sea salt
    (ideally Celtic)
1 pint 6 fl oz (750 ml) fluoride-free,
    lukewarm water

Method
Make the sponge the night before baking. Mix the starter and water together, then add to the flour and mix thoroughly, ideally in a ceramic bowl. Cover with a towel and leave to stand overnight in a warm location. The sponge is ready when it is full of bubbles.

Take a heaped tablespoon of the sponge, mix with a little flour to stiffen, and store in an airtight container such as a jam jar in the refrigerator, where the cold will significantly inhibit the biological activity of the lactic acid bacteria and wild yeasts, preserving the sponge well for 1-2 weeks. Mix the rye flour, wheat flour

and salt together dry in a large bowl. Add some of the water to the remaining sponge, mix to dilute, then add to the flour/salt mixture along with the rest of the water. Knead in the bowl until the ingredients are evenly mixed and the dough can be pulled from the sides of the bowl. It will be fairly stiff. Do not knead more than is required to evenly mix all ingredients: rye flour does not rise properly when kneaded excessively.

Cover with a towel and leave to stand in a warm location for up to three hours. The dough is ready for baking when it has noticeably enlarged and cracked.

Ideally, this bread should be baked in a wood-fired oven. When baking in a conventional oven, use a baking stone (with parchment paper) and cover the loaf with a casserole dish or ceramic crock to imitate the effects of a wood-fired oven. Bake for 20 minutes in an oven preheated to 475°F (250°C/gas 9), 60 minutes at 375°F (190°C/gas 5) and 10 minutes with the oven shut off to simulate the falling temperatures of a masonry oven. Leave to cool for a day on a rack as this kind of bread does not develop a fully matured flavour for at least one day after baking.

For a huge flavour, add 2 tablespoons caraway seeds, 1 tablespoon coriander seeds, 1 teaspoon anise seeds, 1 teaspoon fennel seeds and ½ teaspoon ground cardamom.
(*Adapted from a recipe in* Biologisch kochen und backen *by Helma Danner.*)

Endnote

Our lawns and meadows are a tremendous, largely untapped resource for feeding ourselves and reducing our impact on the planet. Perennial grass plantings, be they lawns or meadows, managed properly, have the potential to act as a carbon sink as mowed grass plants shed roots with each cutting. The carbon from the shed roots is converted to castings by worms and becomes part of the soil. When these plants are consistently mown or grazed at the right time, carbon sequestration is maximized. You have the power to participate in this process by mowing with the scythe and this is just the start.

Pick up your scythe and make hay from your lawn to trade with someone who has animals for milk. Use your scythe to harvest small grains in part of your garden and get chickens to turn the grain (and your kitchen scraps and bugs in your garden) into eggs and meat. Swap your lawnmower or maybe

even your small tractor for a scythe and use the cuttings for sheet mulching which will allow you to grow more of your own food without importing fertility and increase your soil's organic matter. Pick up your scythe and start composting for real; add meaning to your life; and spend more time outdoors. Get to know your mind, body and environment and join with other scythe owners to mow larger and larger areas and have more fun. Above all, have more fun.

A dozen years ago I only knew about scythes from pictures. Now I've eaten my own bread from grains that I grew and harvested, baked in an oven that I built myself. It's made me feel alive in a way that I previously only knew through music. I hope I've given you a starting point to experience something similar, too.

You'll be able to mow larger parcels of land and have more fun when you scythe together with others.

CHAPTER 10 FURTHER INFORMATION AND RESOURCES

As you have seen, there is a lot more to the scythe than simply acquiring one and swinging it. You've got to know how to use it, which in turn means knowing how to use yourself. You've got to know what to use if for, which means knowing what you and your garden need. And you've got to know what you'll do with what you've mown, which means knowing about livestock needs, composting and fermentation. The resources and suppliers listed here may prove useful as your interest in scything develops. This book stands on the shoulders of many other insightful works and I encourage you to seek them out as they expand greatly on subjects that I only touched upon.

Suggested reading and bibliography

ALTERNATIVE AGRICULTURE

Gliessman, Stephen, 2015. *Agroecology: The Ecology of Sustainable Food Systems*. 3rd ed. Boca Raton, FL: CRC Press/Taylor & Francis Group.

Manning, Richard, 2004. *Against the Grain: How Agriculture Has Hijacked Civilization*. New York: North Point Press.

Pollan, Michael, 2008. 'Farmer in Chief' *New York Times Magazine*.
Available at: http://michaelpollan.com/articles-archive/farmer-in-chief/

BREAD, SPROUTING, FERMENTATION

Denzer, Kiko, 2007. *Build Your Own Earth Oven*. 3rd ed. Blodgett, OR: Hand Print Press.

Fallon, Sally, 1999. *Nourishing Traditions*. Washington, DC: New Trends Publishing, Inc.

Katz, Sandor Ellix, 2003. *Wild Fermentation*. White River Junction, VT: Chelsea Green Publishing.

Robertson, Laurel, 2003. *The Laurel's Kitchen Bread Book*. New York: Random House.

Wing, Daniel, 1999. *The Bread Builders*. White River Junction, VT: Chelsea Green Publishing.

ECOLOGICAL SOIL PREPARATION

Jacke, Dave, with Eric Toensmeier, 2005. *Edible Forest Gardens* Vols. I & II. White River Junction, VT: Chelsea Green Publishing.

Jeavons, John, 2012. *How to Grow More Vegetables (and Fruits, Nuts, Berries, Grains, and Other Crops) Than You Ever Thought Possible on Less Land Than You Can Imagine*. 8th ed. Berkeley: Ten Speed Press.

Lanza, Patricia, 1998. *Lasagna Gardening : A New Layering System for Bountiful Gardens*. Emmaus, PA: Rodale Press.

Lee, Andy, and Patricia Foreman, 2011. *Chicken Tractor: The Permaculture Guide to Happy Hens and Healthy Soil*. Good Earth Publications, Inc.

Magdoff, Fred and Harold van Es, 2000. *Building Soils for Better Crops*. Burlington, VT: Sustainable Agriculture Publications.

Nelson, Gary L, 1975. 'Use Pigs' Natural Abilities When Digging a Garden.' *Mother Earth News*.
Available at: http://www.motherearthnews.com/homesteading-and-livestock/digging-a-garden-zmaz75sozgoe.aspx

GRAINS

Heistinger, Andrea, 2013. *The Manual of Seed Saving*. Portland, OR: Timber Press.

Lazor, Jack, 2013. *The Organic Grain Grower*. White River Junction, VT: Chelsea Green Publishing.

Madigan, Carleen, ed. 2009. *The Backyard Homestead*. North Adams, MA: Storey Pub.

Pitzer, Sara, 1981. *Whole Grains*. Charlotte, VT: Garden Way Publishing.

GRASS & HAY

Savory, Allan, and Jody Butterfield, 1999. *Holistic Management*. Washington, DC: Island Press.

Schwenke, Karl, 1991. *Successful Small-Scale Farming: An Organic Approach*. Pownal, VT: Storey Communications.

Voisin, André, 1959. *Grass Productivity*. Washington, DC: Island Press.

MEDITATION, NEUROPLASTICITY AND MIND-BODY CONNECTION

Benson, Herbert, 1992. *The Relaxation Response*. New York: Wings Books.

Davidson, Richard, 2012. *The Emotional Life of Your Brain*. New York: Hudson Street Press.

Mate, Gabor, 2011. *When the Body Says No*. Hoboken, NJ: J. Wiley.

NEEDS-BASED APPROACH TO LIFE

Charter, S.P.R., 1962. *Man on Earth: A Preliminary*

Evaluation of the Ecology of Man. Sausalito, CA: Angel Island Publications.

Hart, Sura, and Victoria Kindle Hodson, 2006. *Respectful Parents, Respectful Kids*. Encinitas, CA: PuddleDancer Press.

Rosenberg, Marshall, 2015. *Nonviolent Communication: A Language of Life*. Encinitas, CA: PuddleDancer Press.

SCYTHES & SCYTHING

Tresemer, David, 2001. *The Scythe Book*. 2nd ed. Chambersberg, PA: A.C. Hood.

Vido, Peter. Numerous articles available at: www.scytheconnection.com

THATCH

Billet, Michael, 1979. *Thatching and Thatched Buildings*. London: Robert Hale Limited.

Fearn, Jacqueline, 2004. *Thatch and Thatching*. Buckinghamshire, UK: Shire Publications, Ltd.

USE OF THE SELF

Dreyer, Danny, 2004. *ChiRunning: A Revolutionary Approach to Injury-Free Running*. New York: Simon & Schuster.

Gokhale, Esther, 2008. *Eight Steps to a Pain-Free Back: Natural Posture Solutions for Pain in the Back, Neck, Shoulder, Hip, Knee and Foot*. Stanford, CA: Pendo Press.

Podulke-Smith, Laurel. 'Constructive Rest' and other articles. Available at: http://www.expandingself.com/constructive_rest

Vineyard, Missy, 2007. *How You Stand, How You Move, How You Live: Learning the Alexander Technique to Explore Your Mind-Body Connection and Achieve Self-Mastery*. New York: Marlowe & Co.

GERMAN-LANGUAGE BOOKS ON SCYTHES, HAY-MAKING AND GRAINS

Aufhammer, Walter, 1998. *Getreide- und andere Körnerfruchtarten*. Stuttgart: Eugen Ulmer Verlag.

Baur, Georg, 1937. *Neuzeitlicher Getreidebau*. Stuttgart: Eugen Ulmer Verlag.

Danner, Helma, 2004. *Biologisch kochen und backen*. Berlin: Ullstein Taschenbuch.

Geith, Richard, 1935. *Die sichere Heuernte*. Berlin: Verlag Paul Parey.

Landis, J., 1933. *Die verbesserte Dürrfutterernte*. Bern: Verbandsdruckerei A.G. Bern.

Lehnert, Bernhard, 2010. *Dengeln und Wetzen: Die Kunst, Sense und Sichel zu schärfen*. Norderstedt, Germany: Books on Demand GmbH.

Lehnert, Bernhard, 2000. *Naturerlebnis: Mähen mit der Sense*. Walsheim, Germany: Edition Europa.

Merzenich, Margret and Erika Thier, 2003. *Brot backen*. Stuttgart: Eugen Ulmer Verlag.

Möller, Rainer, 1988. *Die Sensenschmiede*. Bonn: Rheinland Verlag.

Moser, Heiner, 1988. *Der schweizerische Getreidebau und seine Geräte*. Bern: Haupt.

Niemann, Henning, 1998. *Begleitpflanzen im ökologischen Getreidebau*. Dürkheim, Germany: Stiftung Ökologie & Landbau.

Resch, Andreas, 1995. *Der alpenländische Sensenindustrie um 1900*. Vienna: Böhlau Verlag.

Ries, Ludwig-Wilhelm, 1933. *Getreideernte*. Berlin: Verlag Paul Parey.

Stauch, Fritz.,1933. *Der Getriedebau*.

Wiesauer, Karl, 1999. *Handwerk am Bach: Von Mühlen, Sägen, Schmieden . . . .* Innsbruck: Verlagsanstalt Tyrolia.

Zeitlinger, Josef, 1944. *Sensen, Sensenschmiede und ihre Technik*. Linz, Austria: *Jahrbuch des Vereins für Landeskunde und Heimatpflege im Gau Oberdonau* (previously known as *Jahrbuch des oberösterreichischen Musealvereines*) Vol. 91, Pp. 13-178.

Resources & Supplies

SCYTHES, WHETSTONES, PEENING EQUIPMENT
USA
One Scythe Revolution, Botan Anderson
Falci scythes, Schröckenfux scythes
onescytherevolution.com

Scythe Supply
Schröckenfux scythes
scythesupply.com

Lehman's Hardware
Schröckenfux scythes
lehmans.com

UK
Simon Fairlie (Scythes)
Schröckenfux scythes
thescytheshop.co.uk

Scythe Association
Information, courses, events
scytheassociation.org

SEED
USA
Albert Lea Seeds
Hull-less oats, emmer, rye, hay and pasture mixes,
organic
alseed.com

Bountiful Gardens
Emmer, einkorn, spelt, khorasan wheat, Maris Widgeon
wheat, hull-less barley, hull-less oats, rye, winter wheat,
flax, organic
bountifulgardens.org

Fedco Seeds
Emmer, hull-less oats, hay and pasture mixes, rye,
winter wheat, organic
fedcoseeds.com/ogs/

Johnny's Seeds
Employee-owned, hull-less oats, green manure mixes,
organic
johnyseeds.com

KUSA Seed Society
Ancient wheats
ancientcerealgrains.org

Seed Savers Exchange
seedsavers.org

UK
Brown Envelope Seeds
Oats, emmer, einkorn wheat, amaranth, quinoa
brownenvelopeseeds.com

Kings Seeds
Barley, quinoa, wheat, green manure
kingsseeds.com

Organic Gardening Catalogue
organiccatalogue.com

The Brockwell Bake
Heritage spring wheat seed
brockwell-bake.org.uk

The Real Seed Catalogue
Quinoa and amaranth
realseeds.co.uk

GERMANY

Bio-Saatgut

bio-saatgut.de

Grüner Tiger

gruenertiger.de

SWITZERLAND

Samengärtnerei Zollinger

zollinger-samen.ch

Sativa

sativa-rheinau.ch

GRAIN HARVESTING EQUIPMENT

Treadle-Powered Thresher

The Back to the Land Store

http://www.backtotheland.com/html/wheat_thrasher.html

Seed Winnower

Plans for a hand-operated winnower

saveseeds.org/tools/tool_winnower_hand.html

Grain Huller

Plans for a hand-operated grain huller

savingourseeds.org/pdf/grain_dehuller.pdf

Grain Mills

Lehman's Hardware

Diamant grain mill with heavy cast-iron flywheel for ease in grinding (imitators with aluminum flywheels are much more difficult to turn)

lehmans.com

Osttiroler stone mills

getreidemuehlen.com

Arabella stone mills

familygrainmill.com

Kitchen Aid grain mill attachment

kitchenaid.com

USE OF THE SELF

Alexander Technique

American Society of the Alexander Technique

amsatonline.org

The Society of Teachers of the Alexander Technique

alexandertechnique.co.uk

Meditation

Transcendental Meditation

tm.org

Mindfulness-Based Stress Reduction (MBSR)

umassmed.edu/cfm/stress-reduction/

Zen Monastery Peace Center

livingcompassion.org

Index

THE SCYTHING HANDBOOK

Acknowledgements

Over the years, I have received lots of help from a lot of people with my various scything endeavours, from providing a place to crash, giving me rides, and providing psychological support and inspiration to giving me a place to develop my skills, helping me build a grain cradle, grain thresher and harvest grains, and providing crucial background information. These people include: my parents Susan & John Miller, David & Perry-O Sliwa, the Dörfler family, Gerhard Aichwalder, Michael Kerschbaumer, Ulla Weisshuhn, Andrea Pribil, Susanne Rainer, Janina Thausing, Tommy Baar, the staff of the BOKU library in Vienna, Matthias Rammerstorfer, Johanna Pühringer, Igor Gross, Daniela Fheodoroff, Lelo Brossmann, Daniel Hinteregger, Dietmar Benedetti, Klaus Eberle, Julia Steiner (DkfA), Nina Schreiber, Sensenverein Österreich, Schroeckenfux, Kiko Denzer, Botan Anderson, Chris Wasta, Dave Jacke, David Paquette & Deneb Woods, Ted Wilson, Cindy Ballard, Mary Moody, Rick Mihm, Ashley Neisis, Carolyn Scherf, Michael Phillips, Steve Peterson, Hannah Breckbill, Laurel Podulke-Smith, Tim Galarneau, Jenee Sallee, Louise Hansen, Janna Hoadley, Sandra Menzel, Cristiana Shaw, Kristin Hock, Iantha Rimper, Danielle Ackley, Greg Allen, Tim & Caroline Parker, Steve & Megan Bair.

Picture Acknowledgements

Illustrations on pages 22, 23, 24, 25, 26, 27, 28, 29, 30, 31, 32, 35, 36, 37, 38, 42, 43, 48, 54, 55, 56, 57, 60, 62, 63, 65, 66, 67, 69, 91, 98, 99, 101, 102, 104, 122-3, 124, 125, 127 by Sandra Pond.

Historical illustrations in Chapter 7 reproduced by kind permission of Gesellschaft für Landeskunde und Denkmalpflege, Linz, Austria.

Illustration on page 102 from *Grass Productivity* by André Voisin. Copyright © 1959 by Philosophical Library Inc. (Island Press Edition 1988). Reproduced by permission of Island Press, Washington, DC

Photographs: front cover and pages 3, 6-7, 18-19 Biancardi/Shutterstock; page 2 Andy Cash/Shutterstock; page 39, 126, 144 David Cavagnaro; page 57 Halfpoint/Shutterstock; page 53 Aigars Rheinhold/Shutterstock; pages 11, 132-3 Sensenverein Österreich; pages 121, 129 Andrea Pribil.

About the author

Ian Miller was born in Dubuque, Iowa, and graduated from the University of California, Santa Cruz, with a degree in environmental studies, emphasis agro-ecology. He worked on biodynamic farms in the Austrian province of Carinthia for two years, was the garden crew leader at Seed Savers Exchange in Decorah, Iowa, and received scything instruction certification from the Sensenverein Österreich (Austrian Scything Association).
He now lives near Decorah, Iowa where, in addition to building a small homestead, he practises stone masonry, teaches workshops, writes, translates and makes music.